Police Powers II

Police Powers II

PAUL F. MCKENNA

President, Public Safety Innovation, Inc.

With a foreword by Commissioner Gwen M. Boniface
President, Canadian Association of Chiefs of Police

Toronto

National Library of Canadian Cataloguing in Publication Data

McKenna, Paul F. (Paul Francis), 1952–
    Police powers II

Includes index.
ISBN 0-13-040697-X

1. Police power—Canada. 2. Police administration—Canada. I. Title.

HV8157.M4195 2003   363.2'068   C2001-903761-9

ISBN 0-13-040697-X

Vice President, Editorial Director: Michael J. Young
Acquisitions Editor: Sophia Fortier
Developmental Editor: John Polanszky
Marketing Manager: Sharon Loeb/Christine Cozens
Production Editor: Cheryl Jackson
Copy Editor: David Handelsman
Production Manager: Wendy Moran
Art Director: Julia Hall
Cover and Interior Design: Dave Mckay
Cover Image: Comstock
Page Layout: Susan Thomas/Digital Zone

1 2 3 4 5   06 05 04 03 02

Printed and bound in Canada.

Dedicated to Simone Weil
The Blazing Light of Grace

CONTENTS

CHAPTER TWO
CIVILIAN OVERSIGHT AND POLICE COMPLAINTS IN CANADA 27

CHAPTER THREE
POLICE DISCIPLINE AND ETHICS 71

CHAPTER FIVE

FIRST NATIONS POLICING IN CANADA 122

CHAPTER SIX

POLICE USE OF FORCE   132

CHAPTER SEVEN
OFFICER SAFETY, STRESS, AND WORKPLACE PROTECTION   146

APPENDIX A

APPENDIX B

FOREWORD

ew would question the observation that issues relating to policing and public safety have taken on a profound importance in the appalling shadow of the horrors of September 11th. In Canada, we have been deeply saddened by the devastatingly violent terrorist attack on our closest neighbours and friends in the United States. However, the magnitude of this tragedy may also give us reason for hope as we reflect on the continuing strength and commitment that exists within the fabric of police services on our continent. Nothing can be permitted to unsettle our respect for, and confidence in, the women and men who provide us with services that secure and promote public safety. The Canadian Association of Chiefs of Police (CACP) has long been dedicated to its position of leadership in promoting progressive change in policing. To that end, the CACP has undertaken many initiatives that advance the purposes of innovative policing. This has included serious efforts directed toward the implementation of Bill C-36 dealing with counter-terrorism, the finalization of a national framework on use of force, and the elaboration of an ethical framework for police executives.

Another facet of the CACP's professional commitment pertains to significant initiatives that are aimed at education and continuous learning. There is an ongoing need for carefully prepared publications that outline and explain the nature and evolution of police powers in Canada. This textbook provides the reader with a timely and up-to-date survey of the current theory and practice as it relates to important topics, including civilian governance, police oversight, police discipline and ethics, police labour relations, and First Nations policing, as well as, police officer safety, stress, and workplace protection. Paul McKenna has brought together a wealth of information relevant to these vital topics and has presented it in a manner designed to benefit those wishing to both broaden and deepen their understanding. A great deal of effort has been invested in bringing together extensive references to the growing literature on policing in Canada and the reader is provided with detailed questions and exercises aimed at exploring these matters in a comprehensive manner.

As the complexity of policing continues to reflect the complexity of the global landscape, our organizations will need to be guided by those who have a critical understanding of police powers as they currently exist in Canada today. This publication has been thoughtfully prepared to advance the learning of those concerned about policing and its role in Canadian society.

Commissioner Gwen M. Boniface
President, Canadian Association of Chiefs of
Police

PREFACE

This text constitutes the second part of the Police Powers series, providing a current, concise, and comprehensive learning resource designed to help students develop a solid understanding of police powers in Canada. Although this text contains the most insightful and up-to-date information available at the time of publication, individuals must realize that the state of Canadian law and its practice are always subject to change. To aid students in building the strong foundation of knowledge necessary for competent policing in a changing world, there is an extensive list of references at the end of each chapter. These resources can help new police officers deepen, enhance, and extend their knowledge as they enter the workforce and encounter the ever-changing requirements of Canadian legislatures (federal and provincial) and courts.

Chapter 1 addresses the concept of civilian governance and accountability in Canada. It considers working definitions of the key concepts: governance and accountability and looks at various forms of civilian governance in Canada, including committees of council, police commissions, and police services boards. This chapter also looks at models of civilian governance in Britain and considers notions of police independence and accountability.

Chapter 2 examines civilian oversight of policing in Canada. The "cycle of police oversight" is discussed along with the general features of an oversight system. The specifics of civilian oversight in Ontario are examined, with particular attention to the Ontario Civilian Commission on Police Services and the Special Investigations Unit. The topic of police complaints is also considered as part of the oversight system, again, with an emphasis on Ontario, and some attention given to other Canadian jurisdictions.

Chapter 3 deals with police discipline and ethics. Various approaches to police discipline are examined, including common offences identified in several police codes of conduct. The increasingly critical topic of police ethics is given some attention, with an emphasis on the recently developed model of ethics developed under the auspices of the Canadian Association of Chiefs of Police.

Chapter 4 looks at police labour relations in the Canadian context. Attention is given to the historical growth of police unions and associations in Canada. The key roles of these organizations are reviewed in relationship to their members and the Canadian justice system at large.

Chapter 5 offers a cursory overview of First Nations policing in Canada. The key elements of the growth and development of on-reserve and off-reserve First Nations policing are summarized. The goals of First Nations self-policing initiatives are outlined, and several First Nations policing organizations in Canada are listed.

Chapter 6 deals with the police use of force. It looks carefully at the recently approved national use of force framework approved in principle by the executive of the Canadian Association of Chiefs of Police and explores some of the elements of the use of force continuum, including lethal, and non-lethal (or, less-than-lethal) options available to Canadian police services.

Chapter 7 concludes this text with an examination of the topics of officer safety, stress, and workplace protection. Here we consider the physiology of stress and some of the difficult demands that characterize police work, including issues like shift work and post-traumatic stress disorder. Some proven stress management techniques are reviewed and the various support systems that have been put in place are also considered.

This textbook includes relevant information and current references in all subject areas, as well as questions for consideration and discussion in each chapter. It seeks to provide both students and instructors with relevant related activities and it is anticipated that these elements can be adapted in a variety of ways that will allow for the consolidation of learning, and the extension of understanding pertinent to the individual topics discussed throughout this publication. The appendices contain administrative guidelines for dealing with officers involved in on-duty shooting situations and model policy on dealing with post-shooting incidents, both developed under the auspices of the International Association of Chiefs of Police.

It is anticipated that this textbook will provide students with information relevant for preparing them to learn more about significant elements pertinent to police powers in Canada. There is every expectation that students will find something to attract their interest and attention as they strive to deepen their knowledge about this essential, and fascinating, public service. This textbook should serve as an inducement to further study of and deeper reflection on the nature of policing in Canada.

ACKNOWLEDGMENTS

What appears on the following pages represents a synthesis of years of learning and experience in and around police organizations in Canada. Over the last two decades, I have been deeply engaged in a variety of activities that could be seen as being directed toward the continuous improvement of policing. This has frequently placed me in circumstances that have afforded me unique insights into how police organizations operate. As a civilian it is often difficult to gain access to certain levels of understanding that reflect the authentic presentation of these organizations. However, as a result of building relationships of trust and respect, I have, over time, come to a deep appreciation of the challenges and complexities of policing. This space provides me with an opportunity to identify, and thereby thank, those individuals who have sustained me in my efforts at learning about the ontology of policing in Canada, or, who have informed the product that now carries the weight of my understanding. All those listed below may have some inkling of their role in the development of this textbook; however, I cannot articulate the depth of my gratitude for their individual gifts.

Christine Silverberg has provided me with the most serious model of what it means to be profoundly committed to the public good. Bill Closs has shown perseverance throughout an extensive and exemplary career in policing and demonstrates how friendship and talent can flourish in this exceedingly difficult professional arena. Leanne Bellegarde Daniels has my deepest respect for her manifold kindness, competence, and dignity. Retired Chief of Police Jim Mathews symbolizes what it means to be an effective and ethical police leader. Also, I would like to extend my sincerest thanks to several individuals whose kind assistance has made the solitary labour of writing more productive. Commissioner Gwen Boniface and Angie Howe, on behalf of the Canadian Association of Chiefs of Police, have been gracious in their assistance. William Gibson, Toronto Police Service, has facilitated my access to materials prepared under the auspices of the Canadian Association of Chiefs of Police. Peter Tinsley, Joseph Martino, and Rose Hong of the

Special Investigations Unit have been notably cooperative and generous with regard to this project. Dale Kinnear and Sari Velichka from the Canadian Police Association were helpful in providing me with access to photographs of the Police and Peace Officers' National Memorial Day ceremony. Mike Weaver has contributed his photographic talents to these pages. Sophia Fortier, John Polanszky, and Cheryl Jackson of Pearson Education Canada have, yet again, provided this author with support, guidance, and encouragement, along with David Handelsman, my patiently proficient copyeditor. Finally, I reserve my deepest gratitude for the gentleness of my wife, Lee, and the *thumos* of my daughter, Kathleen.

CHAPTER ONE

CIVILIAN GOVERNANCE AND POLICE ACCOUNTABILITY IN CANADA

LEARNING OBJECTIVES

1. Identify three key models of civilian governance that exist in Canada.
2. Define governance as it pertains to policing in Canada.
3. Define accountability as it pertains to policing in Canada.
4. Describe the distinction between public accountability and operational independence as it relates to modern policing.
5. Identify basic forms of police governing authority in Great Britain.
6. List six key issues relevant to civilian governance in Canada.

INTRODUCTION

This chapter will consider the concepts of civilian governance and police accountability from a broad, overall perspective. The basic elements of governance and accountability will be reviewed to allow the reader to understand the context in which individual oversight mechanisms operate in Canadian policing. This presentation will prepare the reader for a more detailed discussion in Chapter 2, where specific approaches to civilian oversight of policing in Canada will be examined. The whole area of police discipline and ethics will be dealt with in Chapter 3.

In examining some of the fundamental principles that guide the policing function in Canada, it is important to arrive at a sound understanding of the nature of governance and accountability as they impact on police organizations across the country. Because there is a strong connection between Canadian theory and practice in the area of governance and accountability, and British theory and practice, some attention will also be paid to the models in place in Great Britain.

In very general terms, there are three, key models of civilian governance in Canada. They can be identified according to the following categories:

- Committees of council;
- Provincial police commissions; and
- Municipal police commissions and boards.

We will look at these categories of civilian governance in more detail below and consider specific examples of each of these three models. However, it is essential that the context of governance and accountability be considered in advance of this discussion.

WHY CIVILIAN GOVERNANCE?

Why is there a need for civilian governance in Canada? Other professions (e.g., law, medicine, and teaching) are essentially self-regulating. While their governing bodies may include public representatives, they tend to enjoy the privilege of substantial self-governance. Policing in Canada, on the other hand, has been guided by a tradition of governance whereby public representatives fulfill the functions normally associated with governance. As noted in a background document prepared in advance of the police summit hosted by the Ontario Ministry of the Solicitor General and Correctional Services in 1996:

> The structure of civilian governance for police services seeks to ensure that, on one hand, the police remain sufficiently independent in their responsibility for operational matters within their jurisdiction, while, on the other hand, being suitably accountable to representative civilian authorities (e.g., Police Services Boards) for their overall adequacy and effectiveness. (p. 44)

It is important to emphasize the significant balance that is underlined in the above reference. There is general acceptance that police organizations must be permitted to retain a high degree of independence in making determinations about their specific operational commitments and activities. The notion of civilian governance is not intended to reach into those areas of the police function that deal with day-to-day concerns, but rather to oversee the broader areas of policy and procedure that may be considered more strategic in nature. It is essential that civilian governing authorities establish clear parameters within which police organizations can function to effectively meet the needs of the community. Essentially, police services in Canada have been governed by civilian authorities in order to satisfy considerations of the public interest.

There has been an ongoing tension between the concerns for police operational independence and the requirements for governance and accountability (see also Bayley, 1983; Martin, 1995; Ontario. Task Force on Policing in Ontario, 1974; Stenning, 1981a). For example, the 1974 Task Force on Policing in Ontario made the following clear statement:

We adopt the principle that police forces should be independent in their day-to-day operations, yet responsible for overall operations to *elected* representatives. It is our view that through implementation of our role and structural recommendations and through emphasis being placed away from an adversarial relationship between the general public and the police, along with a strong organizational connection to the democratic government structure, citizens' review committees or similar mechanisms are unnecessary. (p. 48) [emphasis added]

We will examine this tension between police independence and public accountability in greater detail later in this chapter. However, in order to consider the nature of this tension, it is helpful to clearly understand the terms that enter into this discussion.

DEFINITION OF GOVERNANCE

Governance relates to the activities associated with the process of "steering" an organization. Governance involves those things that provide an organization with its fundamental sense of direction. The following definition (Leclerc et al., 1996) is useful:

Governance is the exercise of authority, direction and control. It can be thought of as the right and responsibility to determine the purposes and principles by which an organization will function and then to arrange for its management accordingly. The purposes are what the organization seeks to accomplish; the principles are the context, the value system, within which it operates. Governance deals with what an organization is to do and is, therefore, highly focused on planning, setting goals and objectives, and on the development of policies to guide the organization and monitor its progress toward implementation of its plans. (p. 9)

What is important to underline in the above definition is the strategic nature of governance. It is expected that governance bodies operate at a high level on behalf of an organization. The overall planning process, including the setting of goals and objectives, is essential to the well-being of any organization. While the specific programs and activities may vary and change over time, they must always be guided by, and be consistent with, those higher-order goals and objectives that provide the sense of purpose for the organization. It is also valuable to focus on the element in the above definition relating to making provision for the effective management of the organization. Civilian governance does not imply the direct management or administration of the police department. It is certainly possible for modern police organizations to have competent civilian senior managers; however, these individuals will not form part of the civilian governing authority.

DEFINITION OF ACCOUNTABILITY

The next important term to address in this chapter is accountability. If we claim that civilian governance is intended to ensure a high degree of police accountability, what

Chief of police and "chief-for-a-day" with rollerbladers.

do we mean when we speak about accountability? The term is complex; however, it may be understood as follows (Kaufman, 1999):

> This term refers to a requirement that an official give an account to some other person or body with respect to a decision which the official is about to make, is making or has made, or an act that the official is about to do, is doing or has done. The source of such a requirement may vary: it may be the law, it may be an administrative policy, or it may be an established custom or convention....The quintessential modern law dealing with government accountability is 'freedom of information' legislation, which obliges officials to divulge information—sometimes embarrassing—about their activities and decisions. (p. 16)

What is worthy of emphasis in this context is the clear statement that the obligation to provide an account applies even in circumstances where the sharing of embarrassing information is involved. Accountability implies a high standard of responsibility placed on the organization to provide full, frank, and free access to information about all aspects of the organization's operation and activities. Accountability demands that details be forthcoming about the fullest range of an organization's actions, decisions, and expenditures. Again, because the concept of accountability is complex, it is best seen as spanning several dimensions, as Table 1.1 indicates.

There is a strong connection between accountability and the means by which a governing authority can require the achievement of certain goals and objectives. However, it is essential to a clear understanding of the accountability relationship in policing to realize that not all activities can provide guaranteed results. There is a great deal of uncertainty imbedded in the fundamental nature of law enforcement and policing. Police activities, both proactive and reactive, may have some impact on crime rates or on fear of crime levels in any given community, but they cannot ensure precise

TABLE 1.1

DIMENSIONS OF ACCOUNTABILITY

Dimension	Description	Example
Internal & External		
Internal	Accounting flows from the lowest levels to the top in a hierarchical organization. Goals and objectives are defined at the top and communicated to lower levels for action. Authority is delegated accordingly, followed by the rendering of account and possibly the application of a reward system. Generally, such accountability is not public; instead, it remains within management.	Internal audit mechanisms in place in police organizations (e.g., cost centre budgets).
External	Involves a rendering of account by managers to their governing bodies. This rendering of account is public when it takes place, for instance, at the assembly of the people's representatives, the elected body, or when it is directed at stakeholders.	Annual reports prepared by police services for their governing authorities.
Political		
Constitutional	Accountability of the government to Parliament, commonly referred to as ministerial responsibility and generally considered a constitutional requirement.	Solicitors general in the federal and provincial governments.
Decentralized	Establishment of local authorities and regional boards as a response to the overload in a central or a provincial government. This process of decentralization engenders a dispersion of accountability and discourages possible conflicts between the centre and the locality.	Peel Regional Police Services Board.
Consultative	Representative democracy is supplemented by participatory democracy. Elected representatives feel obligated to consult the population; they have a close rapport with special interest groups and even feel a certain accountability to them. Such groups operate outside the electoral process and are not necessarily representative of the broad constituency they claim to represent. The accountability relationships are not clearly defined in such circumstances.	Police/community consultative committees, stakeholders, and special interest groups.

TABLE 1.1 continued

Dimension	Description	Example
Managerial		
Commercial	When government services are financed by user fees rather than by budget appropriation, governments may be judged as much, if not more, on their commercial performance as on the attainment of their public policy purposes. The framework of accountability of many Crown corporations or state enterprises would assume this character.	407/ETR highway in Ontario.
Resource	Accountability for resources is typically indicated for non-market provision of services. Budget-control frameworks must ensure efficiency and be capable of evaluating management performance. Resource accountability can be divided into financial-management accountability; human-resources accountability; and assets-management accountability.	Atomic Energy of Canada Ltd.; Ontario Hydro.
Professional	Allocation of resources in a public institution is often largely influenced, when not decided, by professionals who owe their standards to a self-regulating body. In the name of professional freedom, they appear to operate largely outside democratic control, although they do owe to the legislator the right to exercise their profession.	College of Physicians and Surgeons of Ontario; Ontario College of Teachers, etc.
Legal		
Judicial	Government allows reviews of public servants' actions through judicial reviews of cases brought by aggrieved citizens.	Federal Court of Canada, Commissions of Inquiry.
Quasi-judicial	Accountability takes the form of some body where there is an opportunity for recourse that is not strictly judicial. This will include those bodies that are empowered to apply the law in an administrative capacity, and where there is a large measure of discretion. These bodies operate at arm's length from the political realm. An example of such a special tribunal is the Tax Court of Canada. This is an entity that operates within a quasi-judicial framework of accountability pertaining to tax laws in Canada.	Ontario Civilian Commission on Police Services; RCMP External Review Committee.

TABLE 1.1 continued		
Dimension	**Description**	**Example**
Regulatory	Regulatory agencies are often given a high degree of independence in the application of relatively broad mandates. These mandates are set out in the laws that create such agencies, and they often impact the welfare of individual citizens. Regulatory agencies are empowered to make specified administrative decisions and operate in a manner that is free of direct political interference. This is a complex area of accountability.	Canadian Radio-television and Telecommunications Commission.
Procedural & Consequential		
Procedural	In the sense that if all the input requirements are satisfied, the output, or the intended consequences or results, is deemed assured. Emphasis is on the management procedures, practices, and systems, as well as on compliance to rules and regulations.	Policy and procedure manuals maintained by individual police services.
Consequential	The most significant signals emanate from the monitoring of the output to determine if intended goals have been attained, presumably as a result of the efforts that went into the initiative. Outputs may not all lend themselves to retracing the corresponding inputs. The emphasis is on results, eventual outcomes, and impacts, and constitutes an enlargement of the scope of accountability into what is called effectiveness.	Multi-year business plans prepared by Ontario police services under the new Adequacy Standards Regulation.

Source: Adapted from Leclerc et al. (1996). *Accountability, performance reporting, comprehensive audit: an integrated perspective.* Ottawa: CCAF-FCVI , pp. 57–58.

results in these areas. Police organizations may have influence over only a few of the many variables that represent the root causes of crime and disorder problems in society. The following outlines this reality (Leclerc et al., 1996):

> Accountability depends on a variety of mechanisms that reflect the diversity and complexity of the machinery of government and other public institutions. In such a situation, accountability relationships are not always clear. It is because of this fragmentation that it is important for public bodies to assume their responsibilities and be in a position to explain and justify the manner in which they have discharged their responsibilities. This is essential to the functioning of the democratic political system. (p. 58)

When the notion of accountability is applied to a police service, we arrive at some form of corporate behaviour that meets with the approval of the public at large. Bayley (1983) summarizes the issue:

> An accountable police force shall be taken to be one whose actions, severally and collectively, are congruent with the values of the community in which it works and responsive to the discrepancies when they are pointed out.... clearly, accountability entails the notion of conformability to standards beyond the police, which must refer, in this secular age, to some human community. (p. 146)

Making some clear determinations about the nature of real communities is important to genuine police accountability (McKenna, 2000). Looking at identified needs to set some standards for accountability is critical for the police. Again, Bayley (1983) is helpful in this context:

> The contrivance of accountability involves movement in two directions along the continuum of responsiveness to community control, which makes it plain…that accountability devices cannot be advocated for communities in the abstract, according to a recipe. Particular needs must be assessed, so that changes may be advocated that demonstrate precisely what is thought to be wanting in current police performance. (p. 152)

The movement from an abstract adherence to principles of accountability to the fulfillment of these principles within a living community is vital to quality policing and will determine the efficacy of any given civilian governing authority.

FORMS OF CIVILIAN GOVERNANCE IN CANADA

We have considered working definitions for the terms governance and accountability, and have seen the general applicability of these concepts to policing in Canada. Now it is relevant to examine the actual forms of civilian governance. As noted earlier, there are three models of civilian governance found in Canada:

- Committees of council;
- Provincial police commissions; and
- Municipal police commissions and boards.

There are several variations on the theme of civilian governance that cannot be fully explored in this textbook. Several existing treatments cover the historical background on police commissions and police boards quite admirably (see Stenning, 1981a; Hann et al., 1985). However, the three broad categories discussed below reflect the continuum of civilian governing authorities. In order to gain a full appreciation of the possible range and variety of responsibilities that may fall to a police governing authority, the following list of decision areas is provided (Hann et al., 1985):

- Preparation and/or approval of the police service budget of the force prior to submission to municipal council;
- Authorization of major and/or minor expenditures of the police service;
- Selection of auditors/accountants for the police service;
- Selection of suppliers/contractors/consultants;
- Negotiation and/or final approval of the collective agreement;
- Appointment of the chief of police and/or deputy chief(s);
- Appointment of senior officers other than the chief and deputy chief(s);
- Other promotions within the police service;
- Hiring new members of the police service;
- Establishment of policies and procedures for handling public complaints against members of the police service;
- Dismissal of sworn police officers of the service;
- Dismissal of civilian members of the police service;
- Disposition of disciplinary charges against members of the police service;
- Establishment of general policies for the police service;
- Establishment of overall objectives for the police service;
- Promulgation of rules and regulations for the police service;
- Determination of recruitment policies for police personnel;
- Determination of police personnel selection methods and techniques;
- Determination of the authorized complement for the police service;
- Determination of training, education, and development policies for the police service;
- Determination of whether specific responsibilities should be assigned to uniformed or civilian members within the police service;
- Authorization of the attendance of specific members of the police service at training courses;
- Authorization of official statements and/or press releases to the media;
- Determination of policing strategies (e.g., team policing, high enforcement, foot patrol) to be applied within the police service;
- Determination of whether specialist units should be established within the police service (e.g., drug squad, tactical unit, pawn-shop squad, bicycle patrol);
- Determination of the shift system to be applied within the police service;
- Determination of accommodation to be made available within the police service;
- Determination of general criminal-charging policies; and
- Preparation of the annual report(s) for the police service.

While this may not be an exhaustive list, it does allow some appreciation for the wide scope of responsibilities that may be assumed by a civilian governing authority.

Credit: Special Investigations Unit

SIU investigators recording measurements.

From a strategic perspective, the governing body may have a profound impact on the structure, substance, stability, and character of the police organization for which it is responsible. Accordingly, civilian governance is a subject of pre-eminent importance for policing in Canada.

COMMITTEES OF COUNCIL

The model that holds a police service accountable to a committee of city council is in evidence in several jurisdictions across Canada. It is worth noting, however, that the police service in such circumstances remains distinct from other municipal "departments" due to the special nature of the police officer's status as an officer of the law, as well as the importance of federal and provincial legislation that impacts on law enforcement, public safety, and policing (Stenning, 1981a). However, direct control of policing by a municipal council has often been associated with the worst features of partisan politics and their negative influence on policing, particularly in the United States. This model may also include police services that report directly to a City Manager, rather than to a committee of municipal council.

With the growth of cities in Canada, a need arose for police capabilities that could not be met by the North West Mounted Police, or other provincial police agencies. For example, the *Municipal Institutions of Upper Canada Act, 1858* provided for the establishment of a police force and the regulation of the duties and conduct of officers in Upper Canada. As Stenning (1981a) points out:

> With the gradual development of systems of local elected government…an important change occurred in the government of urban police forces. Instead of being viewed principally as a service

ancillary to the judiciary, police forces increasingly came to be viewed as primarily a municipal service. (p. I.4)

Because municipalities paid for these policing services, they were inclined to apply the "pay-for-say" principle and seek to wield the fullest degree of control over the police department in their jurisdiction.

In order to avoid the dilemma of partisan politics diverting municipal policing from its proper course, special purpose bodies were created in Canada. These were typically referred to as boards of commissioners of police. In fact, Canada has a long tradition of police boards as an institution for the governance of police services within municipalities (Stenning, 1981a; Hann et al., 1985). This pattern may be seen as an early recognition of the need to buffer municipal police departments from the direct control of municipal councils. It is perhaps a tribute to the Canadian spirit of compromise that accountability has, generally, been expressed in the form of a blended model, with municipal and provincial representatives assuming shared responsibility for civilian governance.

PROVINCIAL POLICE COMMISSIONS

Here we are referring to governing bodies that function at the provincial level. A provincial police commission will likely be responsible for all of the police organizations within a province's jurisdiction. An example of such a governing authority is the Ontario Civilian Commission on Police Services, discussed in greater detail below.

With the growth in the practice of contracting with the Royal Canadian Mounted Police as the "provincial" police in all jurisdictions excluding Quebec and Ontario (and to some extent, Newfoundland and Labrador), there arose a need to ensure that individual provinces held some margin of responsibility for the provincial interest in matters pertaining to policing and public safety. Provincial police commissions have been an appropriate mechanism for meeting this need. Stenning (1981a) notes that the pressure for the creation of a provincial police commission also came from the local municipal police associations and has summarized the issue as follows:

> Another major influence over the creation of provincial police commissions in the contract provinces, were the demands both of the police associations representing the rank-and-file members of the municipal police forces, and of the public, for a more uniform and effective handling of police complaints and internal disciplinary matters with respect to municipal police forces. This pressure included demands for the establishment of a uniform code of discipline and disciplinary procedures applicable to all municipal police forces, as well as for the establishment of some independent body which could review and rule on local disciplinary decisions and the local disposition of public complaints against the police. (p. I.108)

Provincial police commissions have been seen as a good means for arriving at certain standard levels of police service. While operational needs would obviously vary from one municipality to another, it was felt that a minimum level of competence was required in the area of policing that could be met only by arriving at agreed-upon standards. Again, Stenning (1981a) is helpful on this point:

> In all these jurisdictions, the adoption of provincial police commissions appears to have been mo-tivated by common objectives: to accomplish greater coordination and efficiency of policing services throughout the province; to establish and impose minimum standards of recruitment, training, discipline and working conditions for police forces; to provide for an independent au-thority to review and decide on local decision-making with respect to internal disciplinary mat-ters and the disposition of public complaints against the police; and to plan and implement an overall police policy for the province. (p. I.117–18)

ONTARIO CIVILIAN COMMISSION ON POLICE SERVICES

At the provincial level in Ontario, the highest expression of accountability for polic-ing is found in the Ontario Civilian Commission on Police Services. This body was orig-inally formed in 1962 and was then known as the Ontario Police Commission. It represents an important aspect of police oversight in Ontario, and we will consider its pivotal role in the area of public complaints and police discipline in Chapter 2. However, from the broad perspective of civilian governance and police accountabil-ity, the Ontario Civilian Commission on Police Services holds an important place in the hierarchy of responsible agencies dealing with policing and law enforcement. Its members are appointed by the Lieutenant Governor in Council, which simply means that all appointments are made at the discretion of the Ontario government. The commission is required to file an annual report, at the end of each calendar year, with the Ontario Solicitor General outlining its affairs and activities.

In November 1997, the *Police Services Amendment Act, 1997* came into force. This represented a significant modification to policing legislation in Ontario and brought about major changes in the public complaints scheme and other aspects rel-evant to the delivery of police services. Part II of the *Police Services Act*, as amended in 1997, contains details pertaining to the roles and responsibilities of the Ontario Civilian Commission on Police Services. Several important elements are set out below:

22.(1) The Commission's powers and duties include,
(a) if the Solicitor General advises the Commission that a board or municipal police force is not complying with prescribed standards of police services,
   (i) directing the board or police force to comply, and
   (ii) if the Commission considers it appropriate, taking measures in accordance with sub-section 23(1);
(b) [REPEALED]
(c) conducting investigations with respect to municipal police matters under section 25;
(d) conducting inquiries into matters relating to crime and law enforcement under section 26;
(e) conducting inquiries, on its own motion, in respect of a complaint or complaints made

about the policies of or services provided by a police force or about the conduct of a police officer and the disposition of such complaint or complaints by a chief of police or board;

(e.1) conducting reviews under section 72, at the request of a complainant, into the decision that a complaint is about the policies of or services provided by a police force or is about the conduct of a police officer, that a complaint is frivolous or vexatious, made in bad faith or unsubstantiated, that the complaint will not be dealt with because it was made more than six months after the facts on which it is based occurred, that the complainant was not directly affected by the policy, service or conduct that is the subject of the complaint or that the misconduct or unsatisfactory work performance was not of a serious nature;

(e.2) making recommendations with respect to the policies of or services provided by a police force by sending the recommendations, with any supporting documents, to the Solicitor General, the chief of police, the association, if any, and, in the case of a municipal police force, the board;

(f) hearing and disposing of appeals by members of police forces and complainants in accordance with Part V. R.S.O. 1990, c. P.15, s. 22(1); 1995, c.4, s.4(3); 1997, c.8, s.16(1-3).

When the commission conducts an investigation or inquiry, it has all the powers of a commission under Part II of the *Public Inquiries Act*. Because the commission has such an important role in the oversight of police services, including matters pertaining to public complaints and officer discipline, we will be taking a more detailed look at the commission's powers and duties in Chapters 2 and 3.

MUNICIPAL POLICE COMMISSIONS AND BOARDS

It may be suggested that civilian governance has reached its furthest stage of evolution in Ontario. With the introduction of the *Police Services Act*, Ontario has developed a system of civilian governance that is aimed at ensuring a high degree of accountability, as well as promoting significant levels of adequacy and effectiveness in policing. This system builds on a tradition of adherence to significant civilian governance within the province.

The *Municipal Institutions of Upper Canada Act, 1858* provided the authority for local (i.e., municipal) governments to operate their respective police departments. However, this legislation required that these police organizations were to be supervised by a body known as a Board of Commissioners of Police. This effectively established the practice of an independent civilian body that could insulate policing and public safety from any risks associated with the direct influence of partisan politics. It may be considered an important social innovation impacting on policing. These boards of commissioners of police were originally composed of three office-holders:

1. the mayor;
2. a recorder; and
3. the police magistrate.

It is important to note that the recorder and the police magistrate were both appointed by the Crown; that is to say, they were appointed by the provincial government. Both members were, *ex-officio*, justices of the peace. Stenning (1981a) places considerable emphasis on the desire of the drafters of this legislation to hold the police aloof from the undue influences of municipal councils by means of the Board of Commissioners of Police:

> The scheme of this legislation makes it quite clear that it was intended that the Board should have a considerable degree of autonomy and independence from the dictates of the municipal council, no matter what its composition may be. The powers and functions of the Board were not powers and functions delegated by the council, but statutory powers and functions conferred directly on the Board itself. (p. I.10)

It was intended that the decisions of the board would not be overly influenced by the interests of municipal council, but legislators recognized the reality that municipal representatives would have to play a significant role in the provision of local services that they funded through municipal taxes.

This effort at compromise has been in evidence in many jurisdictions across Canada and is based upon a common desire for bridging a variety of political and local interests. Stenning (1981a) offers the view that:

> Virtually the only characteristics which all municipal police boards in Canada have in common is that, to a greater or lesser extent, they all represent an alternative to direct governance of municipal police forces by municipal councils. As such, they are, and always will be, highly controversial institutions since to many of their opponents they represent an implied lack of confidence in the competence and integrity of locally elected municipal governments. (p. III.2)

The *Police Services Act* provides a detailed description of the roles and responsibilities of a police services board in Ontario. This model has developed from the original experiment with the Board of Commissioners of Police in the mid-19th century. Further adaptations to this form of governance appeared in the *Police Act* of 1946. With amendments in 1997, the *Police Services Act* required that there be a police services board in every municipality that maintained a police force. All boards of commissioners of police that were already in existence were continued as police services boards. Table 1.2 outlines the various sizes and composition of police services boards authorized by the legislation, based on population size.

It is worth noting that with the amendments to the *Police Services Act* introduced in 1997, the following persons are not eligible to be members of a police services board:

- a judge;
- a justice of the peace;
- a police officer; and
- a person who practises criminal law as a defence counsel.

TABLE 1.2

SIZE AND COMPOSITION OF POLICE SERVICES BOARDS

Population	Board Size	Council Representative	Public Representative	Provincial Appointment
25 000 or less	Three members	One head of council (mayor) or another member of council	One member who is not a member of council nor an employee of the municipality	One member appointed by the Lieutenant Governor in Council
Over 25 000	Five members	One head of council (mayor) or another member of council; one member of council	One member who is not a member of council nor an employee of the municipality	Two members appointed by the Lieutenant Governor in Council
Over 300 000	Seven members	One head of council (mayor) or another member of council; two members of council	One member who is not a member of council nor an employee of the municipality	Three members appointed by the Lieutenant Governor in Council

The following responsibilities of police services boards are taken from the *Police Services Act*:

31.(1) A board is responsible for the provision of adequate and effective police services in the municipality and shall,

(a) appoint the members of the municipal police force;

(b) generally determine, after consultation with the chief of police, objectives and priorities with respect to police services in the municipality;

(c) establish policies for the effective management of the police force;

(d) recruit and appoint the chief of police and any deputy chief of police, and annually determine their remuneration and working conditions, taking their submissions into account;

(e) direct the chief of police and monitor his or her performance;

(f) establish policies respecting the disclosure by chiefs of police of personal information about individuals;

(g) receive regular reports from the chief of police on disclosures and decisions made under section 49 (secondary activities);

(h) establish guidelines with respect to the indemnification of members of the police force for legal costs under section 50;

(i) establish guidelines for dealing with complaints made under Part V;

(j) review the chief of police's administration of the complaints system under Part V and receive regular reports from the chief of police on his or her administration of the complaints system.

TORONTO POLICE SERVICES BOARD

In 1859, the Dominion of Canada established the first Board of Police Commissioners for Toronto, by virtue of the *Municipal Institutions of Upper Canada Act, 1858*, noted above. The mayor, Sir Adam Wilson, was the chairman; George Duggan, the recorder; and George Gurnett, the police magistrate.

In 1956, with the creation of the Municipality of Metropolitan Toronto, a five-member board of commissioners of police was established to oversee the new police department. The model established for this civilian governing authority would serve as a template for other regional jurisdictions that resulted from municipal amalgamations in Ontario during the 1960s and 1970s (Stenning, 1981a). This new police organization was the result of a blending of the existing Toronto Police Force with the police departments from the following areas:

- the townships of East York, Etobicoke, York, Scarborough, and North York;
- the towns of Leaside, Mimico, New Toronto, and Weston; and
- the villages of Forest Hill, Long Branch, and Swansea.

As interest grew within the province of Ontario for regional levels of government, the Metropolitan Toronto Board of Commissioners of Police model became the standard for civilian governance. Regional municipalities came into existence in the following areas:

- Niagara;
- York;
- Sudbury;
- Waterloo;
- Peel;
- Halidmand-Norfolk;
- Halton;
- Hamilton-Wentworth; and
- Durham.

Each of these jurisdictions modelled its civilian governing authorities on the example established by Metropolitan Toronto. Currently, the Toronto Police Service oversees one of the largest municipal police organizations in Canada and continues to function as a blend of municipal and provincial representatives.

VANCOUVER POLICE BOARD

The Vancouver Police Board is the civilian governing authority for the Vancouver Police Department. It includes the mayor of Vancouver, one member appointed by Vancouver City Council, and an additional five members appointed by the province (formally, by the Lieutenant Governor in Council) after consultation with the director of police services (who reports to the Ministry of the Attorney General). The mayor is designated as chair of the police board, and members are chosen to reflect the demographics of the community. They are typically persons who have demonstrated their capacity to act in the best interests of the community.

CALGARY POLICE COMMISSION

This is the civilian body to which the Calgary Police Service is accountable. Members of the commission are volunteers and are appointed by the Calgary City Council to oversee policing in the city. The members of the commission make decisions and issue instructions as a statutory body under the Alberta *Police Act*. The commission has four standing committees: Finance and Budget, Policy and Priorities, Personnel, and Citizen Complaints Review. The committees develop research and recommendations; however, the commission is exclusively empowered to act as a whole to approve a resolution or enact a policy.

The Calgary Police Commission is a link between the community and the police. The commission's mandate is to balance the requirements of public accountability and those of police independence and provide a buffer between the police and partisan political demands. The Alberta *Police Act* gives the commission the responsibility for appointing the chief of police, establishing policing priorities, and allocating funds provided by City Council. The commission issues directions to the Police Service through the chief of police. The chief is responsible for the day-to-day operations of the police service.

The Calgary Police Commission currently employs four civilian staff:

- An executive director;
- A civilian complaints monitor; and
- Two administrative assistants.

The executive director's responsibilities are to:

- Ensure the flow of information among the commission, the citizens of Calgary, the police service, the City of Calgary, and other agencies;
- Provide administrative support and advice on matters of governance and procedure to the members of the commission;
- Ensure that an accurate record is kept of all commission activities; and
- Manage the commission office and staff.

MODELS OF CIVILIAN GOVERNANCE IN BRITAIN

As with many aspects of policing, there are significant parallels between the models of civilian governance applied in Britain and those in evidence in Canada. Table 1.3 provides a summary of those models currently in place in Britain.

TABLE 1.3

FORMS OF POLICE GOVERNING AUTHORITY IN GREAT BRITAIN

Police Service	Police Authority	Comments
Metropolitan Police	Home Secretary	This represents a form of fully centralized accountability.
City of London Police	Common Council of the City	This equates with Canadian jurisdictions that maintain accountability through a committee of municipal council.
English and Welsh counties	Standing Committee comprising equal numbers of elected officials nominated by the county council and justices of the peace elected by quarter sessions	Similar to the earlier model of boards of commissioners of police in Ontario where municipal council appointed members, and the province appointed justices of the peace.
Cities and boroughs in England and Wales	Watch Committee composed of not more than one-third of the council	Also similar to boards of commissioners of police and police services boards.
Scotland	County or burgh council	This equates with Canadian jurisdictions that maintain accountability through a committee of municipal council.
Combined police forces of England and Wales	Ad hoc body generally comprising members of the local authorities whose forces have been combined	Similar to regional police services boards in Ontario (e.g., York Region, Peel Region, Niagara Region, Durham Region, Waterloo Region).

Source: Adapted from Oliver, Ian (1987). *Police, government and accountability*. London: Macmillan Press, p. 26.

There are substantial similarities between the organizational structure of policing in Britain and Canada. This has been accurately observed by Martin (1995):

> The modern police agency bears the structural characteristics of its prototype in Peel's England. It is bureaucratic and rule-bound with chain-of-command control; discipline-centred, with compliance tending to be a qualification for rank while training is not taken seriously. Police are seen to act according to the law, bound by procedure, with legalistic constraints and accountability and oversight that is judicial rather than local or political. They are to operate within the confines of explicit law even during routine order-maintenance tasks. Police are to act with minimal use of force. They are to be relentlessly nonpartisan and insulated from direct political influence. (p. 8)

POLICE INDEPENDENCE VERSUS ACCOUNTABILITY

There has been a longstanding concern with regard to the preservation of police independence and autonomy against unreasonable encroachments by political authorities, at all levels. The argument is normally made that such independence and autonomy are essential if police organizations are to be free from local partisan political interests that might detract from a strict observance of the law. As Martin (1995) indicates:

> Police autonomy evolved from a history of ensuring that policing be free of interference by largely local political or improperly biased interests. In the United States, police chiefs enjoy considerable autonomy even though they are appointed by a mayor and can be readily dismissed. Much of police autonomy, while informal, is politically potent because it is founded on public support for an "apolitical" police force. (p. 142)

While police independence may not negate accountability, it is a subject that has provoked considerable controversy. It has been suggested that authority rests upon a capacity for reasoned elaboration, which implies that those who hold authority must exercise power in a manner that allows for adequate, and reasonable, explanation. Bayley (1983) attempts to understand the confusion that sometimes exists when police perceive accountability as a threat to their independence:

> In many countries, especially the United States, police react automatically against any threat to their fancied independence. They persistently fail to grasp the fact that public trust must be earned, which means someone outside the organisation must be able to check up on them. It has always struck me in the United States that police antipathy to civilians is short-sighted. If most complaints are, as research shows, resolved in favor of the police once the facts are known, then the police have more to gain than lose by responsible investigation attested by non-police people. (p. 158)

It is important to understand that police organizations, especially in Canada where democratic principles inform all public services, must be seen as part of the political realm. Canadian police services inhabit common ground with other agencies, institutions, and departments that serve the public good. To somehow perceive that the police are independent of the rigours, requirements, and obligations of public accountability is to misunderstand the police mandate in Canada. Public accountability is the lifeblood of the political realm within a democratic context. Police services are, therefore, embedded in the political fabric and must accept and acknowledge the sanctions, support, and scrutiny that this entails. Martin (1995) explores the process whereby the police have been "repoliticized" in Canada:

> The repoliticization of policing, making it clearly accountable to local political offices if not placing it under their immediate direction, has found it proponents. The report of the Waterloo Region Review Commission underlines the strength with which the proposition can be made.

> Reasons for keeping politics out of policing, it noted, are largely fraudulent, for however the system may be structured, the police governing body must ultimately be responsible to the public. This, the report continues, is both accountability and politics. (p. 161)

While it is not necessarily the case that police services should be tied tightly to the municipal political level, there is a need to ensure that the broad public interest is reflected in the policies, practices, priorities, and procedures that the police pursue. Again, Martin (1995) summarizes a dilemma that confronts all civilian governing authorities as they attempt to rationalize the degree of engagement they wish to achieve in their oversight function:

> So the conundrum persists: how to arrange police accountability and supervision within a political mix of interests, local and central, while fitting those arrangements into the existing structure of government and the criminal justice system. The time has come to discuss this conundrum [from] the perspective of professionalism. (p. 161)

ACCOUNTABILITY AND POLICE PROFESSIONALISM

Much of the discussion around police independence as it impacts on police accountability involves some reflection on the nature of policing in Canada. Can policing be considered a profession? Does the nature of accountability change as policing in Canada becomes more predictable, more precise, in a word, more professional? The question of whether or not policing in Canada is a true profession involves considerations which are well beyond the immediate scope of this textbook. However, it is relevant to a sound understanding of the topics treated in this publication to address some of the concerns that are raised in the context of this question.

The issue of the threat to longstanding police unionism in the face of growing professionalization of the police service in Canada is addressed by Martin (1995):

> Leonard O. Gertler and Ronald W. Crowley characterized professionalism as the joining of competence and advanced technology to the ideals of social service and social justice. The professionalization of occupations is a widely accepted, common method by which to ensure their continued competence, and accountability, in serving the vital interests of clients. In the modern context, a nonprofessionalized police occupation is an anomaly. The issue of police professionalization bears directly on their occupational competence, responsiveness to societal needs, accountability, and capacity to evolve. (p. 170)

In the professional model exemplified by August Vollmer and articulated by James Q. Wilson, there is some degree of separation from the public when the police self-consciously label themselves as "professional." A comparison may be made to the scientific, medical, or technical models, where those introduced to the complexities of their discipline possess a specialized knowledge that the average person would not comprehend and, therefore, cannot judge. Brown (1988) shares the following insight into the difficulty associated with this perspective, particularly if one considers the philosophy of community policing, rightly understood:

> A professional police force does not serve a community by responding to the unique and particular needs of its different segments; rather the police serve by controlling crime and enforcing the law in the community as a whole. The police are more than servants, they are professional servants. They stand above the community and assume responsibility for interpreting and judging what are the serious problems of crime and disorder that a community faces and what should be done about them. (p. 56)

It is doubtful that Canadians would consent to a model of policing where police officers occupy a position above the community and are empowered to independently judge the problems of crime and disorder, arriving at their own solutions to these problems. Our principles compel us to place a higher premium on accountability than professionalism, if that professionalism will somehow remove the practitioners from a close relationship with the citizens they serve. The importance Canadians place on civilian governance favours accountability over professionalism; however, we continue to support the highest standards of excellence in the pursuit of quality policing. Of particular relevance in this context is the need to ensure that front-line officers possess the best skills, aptitudes, and abilities when pursuing the discipline of policing. Stinchcombe (1980) emphasizes the need to pay close attention to the operational police officer, the person who most often, and most directly, impacts the public:

> [P]rofessionalism in the true sense of the word can only occur from the bottom up—it must be perceived as a vehicle for self-growth by the officers themselves, rather than an imposition by those in authority, in order to be really effective. Only when the existing fear of authority is replaced by a personal commitment on the part of entry-level employees will an environment emerge in which professionalism can grow and be nourished. (p. 60)

Another related issue concerns the possibility of combining increasing professionalization with police unionism. Police associations characterize themselves as being representatives of the workers within police departments and in opposition to management, but this is not always the reality. Professionalism implies a high-level practitioner who functions in a collegial manner, with little or no hierarchy within the professional category. The practices associated with unionism do not integrate easily with the professional model. This reality is reflected by Martin (1995):

> In the context of the postindustrial society, the continuing professionalization of the workplace poses long-term questions about the union movement, whose membership has declined over the years, except, significantly, in public-sector unions. The entry of young, educated workers may well challenge both the common organization work and its character, and the structures of trade unionism and professional organizations. (p. 200)

THE FUTURE OF CIVILIAN GOVERNANCE IN CANADA

As policing in Canada evolves it is certain that civilian governance will likewise continue to develop. Consistent with our democratic principles and our adherence to fundamental justice, police organizations will be held accountable for their actions, both administrative and operational. However, if civilian governance is to remain responsible to the public interest and worthy of respect, there are several issues that must continue to be of importance:

• Selection of qualified governing authority members;
• Orientation, training, development, and continuing education of governing authority members;
• Openness of governing authority meetings;
• Openness of governing authority hearings;
• Access to governing authority documents; and
• Representativeness of governing authorities.

CONCLUSION

This chapter has considered the overall topic of civilian governance and its relationship to general principles of accountability. The existence of three basic models of governing bodies has been reviewed, and there has been some discussion regarding the importance of civilian governance in the context of policing in Canada.

In order to facilitate a deeper understanding of the range of accountability mechanisms, this chapter has concentrated on some of the topical areas that have been identified in the relevant literature and applied them to Canadian policing.

We have outlined, in a general fashion, the major forms of civilian governance in Canada. Several examples have been included in this chapter. However, it is essential that broader study supplement what can only be a cursory presentation in this treatment. It should be clear, in any event, that Canada, especially Ontario, has a deep and abiding commitment to the principle and practice of civilian governance. There is reference to the range of approaches currently in place in Great Britain, and it is, therefore, possible to see parallels between that jurisdiction and our own in terms of civilian governance.

This chapter has explored the complex, and frequently highly contentious, issue of police independence and its relationship to accountability. We have also made some reference to police professionalism in a similar context. All of the matters addressed in this chapter have been framed in preparation for a more detailed examination of civilian oversight of policing that follows in Chapter 2.

QUESTIONS FOR CONSIDERATION AND DISCUSSION

1. How is it possible to balance political accountability with operational independence in a modern police service?
2. Which of the three models for civilian governance in Canada appears to function most effectively?
3. What are the advantages and disadvantages of greater centralization of civilian governance? Compare the models of governance in place in both Canada and Britain on this topic.
4. How do police services boards differ from committees of municipal council in the context of civilian governance in Canada?

RELATED ACTIVITIES

1. Select two jurisdictions with different forms of civilian governance in Canada and compare the structure and organization of those bodies.
2. Research the debates that took place during the sessions of the Ontario Legislature leading up to the creation of the Ontario Police Commission (the precursor to the existing Ontario Civilian Commission on Police Services). They can be found in the *Legislative Debates* 22 November 1961, p. 7.
3. Review the ongoing work of the Ontario Civilian Commission on Police Services over the past two years and comment on the various issues and concerns it has addressed.
4. Compare the governance of policing in Canada, or any of the individual provinces, with the governance of some other professional group (e.g., lawyers, doctors, teachers, or engineers). How do these groups differ in their structure, mandate, goals, and objectives?
5. Pick one specific civilian governing authority and fully research its creation, composition, mandate, roles, and responsibilities.

REFERENCES

Andrews, Allen H. Jr. (1985). "Structuring the political independence of the police chief." In Geller, William A. (ed.) *Police leadership in America: crisis and opportunity*. New York: Oxford University Press.

Aucoin, P. (1978). Public accountability in the governing professions: a report on the self-governing professions of accounting, engineering and law in Ontario. Unpublished working paper, Dalhousie University.

Bayley, D.H. (1983). "Accountability and control of the police: some lessons for Britain." In Bennett, T. (ed.) *The future of policing: papers presented to the 15th Cropwood Round-Table Conference December 1982*. Cambridge: Institute of Criminology, University of Cambridge.

Bennett, T. (ed.) (1983). *The future of policing: papers presented to the 15th Cropwood Round-Table Conference December 1982.* Cambridge: Institute of Criminology, University of Cambridge.

Brown, M.K. (1988). *Working the street: police discretion and the dilemma of reform.* New York: Russell Sage Foundation.

Ceyssens, Paul, Susan C. Dunn, and Scott Childs (2000). *Ontario Police Services Act fully annotated, 2000-2001 edition.* Saltspring Island, B.C.: Earlscourt Press.

Childs, Scott and Paul Ceyssens (1998). "Doe v. Metropolitan Toronto Board of Commissioners of Police and the status of public oversight of the police in Canada." *Alberta Law Review,* Vol. 36, p. 1000.

Epstein, Joyce and Sheila Vanderhoef (1977). *Paraprofessionalism: a study for the Winnipeg Police Commission.* Winnipeg: Institute of Urban Studies, University of Winnipeg.

Hann, Robert G. et al. (1985). "Municipal police governance and accountability in Canada: an empirical study." *Canadian Police College Journal,* Vol. 9, no. 1, pp. 1–85.

Hudson, J. (1971). "Police review boards and police accountability." *Law and Contemporary Problems,* Vol. 36, pp. 515–538.

Hudson, J. (1972). "Organizational aspects of internal and external review of the police." *Journal of Criminal Law, Criminology and Police Science,* Vol. 63, pp. 427–433.

Jefferson, T. and R. Grimshaw (1982). "Law, democracy and justice: the question of police accountability." In Cowell, D., T. Jones and J. Young (eds.) *Policing the riots.* London: Junction Books.

Jefferson, T. and R. Grimshaw (1984). *Controlling the constable: police accountability in England and Wales.* London: Muller.

Kaufman, The Honourable Fred (1999). *Review of the Nova Scotia Public Prosecution Service: final report.* Halifax: Province of Nova Scotia.

Leclerc, Guy et al. (1996). *Accountability, performance reporting, comprehensive audit: an integrated perspective.* Ottawa: CCAF-FCVI.

Littlejohn, E. (1981). "The civilian police commission: a deterrent of police misconduct." *University of Detroit Journal of Urban Law,* Vol. 59, pp. 5–59.

Lustgarten, L. (1986). *The governance of police.* London: Sweet and Maxwell.

Maloney, Arthur (1975). *The Metropolitan Toronto review of citizen-police complaint procedure: report to the Metropolitan Toronto Board of Commissioners of Police.* Toronto: Metropolitan Toronto Board of Commissioners of Police.

Martin, Maurice A. (1995). *Urban policing in Canada: anatomy of an aging craft.* Montreal and Kingston: McGill-Queen's University Press.

McDougall, A.K. (1971). Law and politics: the case of police independence in Ontario. Unpublished paper presented to 43rd annual meeting of the Canadian Political Science Association. June.

McDougall, A.K. (1971). Policing in Ontario: the occupational dimension to provincial-municipal relations. Unpublished doctoral thesis, University of Toronto.

McKenna, Paul F. (2000). *Foundations of Community Policing in Canada.* Scarborough, Ont.: Pearson Education Canada.

Oliver, Ian (1987). *Police, government and accountability.* London: Macmillan Press.

Ontario. Ministry of the Solicitor General and Correctional Services (1996). *Policing Ontario: building for the future: June 8th & 9th, 1996.* Toronto: Ministry of the Solicitor General and Correctional Services.

Ontario. Secretariat for Social Development (1984). *Police governing authorities in Ontario: two centuries of service.* Toronto: The Secretariat.

Ontario. Task Force on Policing in Ontario (1974). *The Task Force on Policing in Ontario: report to the Solicitor General*. Toronto: The Task Force.

Ontario. Waterloo Region Review Commission (1978). *Police governance in Waterloo Region*. Toronto: Queen's Printer.

Oppal, The Honourable Mr. Justice Wallace T. (1994). *Closing the gap: policing and the community: the report, volume 1*. [Victoria, B.C.]: Policing in British Columbia Commission of Inquiry.

Pollard, Brian (1983). "Police effectiveness and public acceptability." In Bennett, T. (ed.) *The future of policing: papers presented to the 15th Cropwood Round-Table Conference December 1982*. Cambridge: Institute of Criminology, University of Cambridge.

Shearing, C. (ed.) (1981). *Organizational police deviance*. Toronto: Butterworths.

Simmonds, R.H. (1982). "An address to the International Conference on police accountability." *Canadian Police College Journal*, Vol. 6, no. 3, pp. 179–187.

Stenning, Philip C. (1981a). *Police commissions and boards in Canada*. Toronto: Centre of Criminology, University of Toronto.

Stenning, Philip C. (1981b). "The role of police boards and commissions as institutions of municipal police governance." In Shearing, Clifford D. (ed.) *Organizational police deviance: its structure and control*. Toronto: Butterworths.

Stenning, Philip C. (ed.) (1995). *Accountability for criminal justice: selected essays*. Toronto: University of Toronto Press.

Stinchcombe (1980). "Beyond bureaucracy: a reconsideration of the 'professional' police." *Police Studies*, Vol. 3, no. 1, pp. 49–61.

Waterloo Region Review Commission (1978). *Police governance in Waterloo Region*. Toronto: Queen's Printer.

RELEVANT CASE LAW

Attorney General for New South Wales v. Perpetual Trustee Company Limited, [1955] A.C. 477

Jowitt et al. v. Board of Commissioners of Police of City of Thunder Bay (1974), 3 O.R. (2d) 95

Mahood v. Hamilton-Wentworth Regional Board of Police Commissioners et al. (1977), 14 O.R. (2d) 708

R. v. Commissioner of Police ex parte Blackburn, [1968] 1 All E.R. 763

R. v. Metropolitan Toronto Board of Commissioners of Police ex parte Prosser, [1971] 3 O.R. 363, 20 D.L.R. (3d) 403 (C.A.)

Ramsay v. the Chief of Police for Metropolitan Toronto et al. (1988), 66 O.R. (2d) 99

Re A Reference Under the Constitutional Questions Act (1957), O.R. 28

Re Brown and Waterloo Regional Police Commissioners Board and Ontario Police Commission (1980), 13 C.R. (3d) 46, (1980), 28 O.R. (3d) 737, (1981), 31 O.R. (2d) 417

Re Metropolitan Toronto Board of Commissioners of Police, [1973] 30 O.R. 563, 37 D.L.R. (3d) 487 (Div. Ct.)

Re Metropolitan Toronto Police Association and Metropolitan Board of Commissioners of Police (1975), 4 O.R. (2d) 83, 5 O.R. (2d) 285

Re Nicholson and Haldimand-Norfolk Regional Board of Commissioner of Police (1978), 88 D.L.R. (3d) 671 (S.C.C.)

WEBLINKS

 www.gov.calgary.ab.ca/cpc The Calgary Police Commission website provides general information on topics like safety and crime prevention, information for kids and teens to help them make informed decisions, and information on becoming an officer.

 www.torontopoliceboard.on.ca The Toronto Police Services Board is a civilian board that oversees the provision of police services in Toronto, including law enforcement and crime prevention. With its frequently asked questions section and a link to the Toronto Police Service Employment Unit, this site is a great resource for both new and experienced officers.

 www.city.vancouver.bc.ca/police/policeboard The Vancouver Police Board's website lists its members and explains the board's functions. There are links to the city's homepage and to a map of Vancouver.

 www.aclc.net/submissions/police_accountability.html The African Canadian Legal Clinic's website offers information on police accountability, specifically in relation to the Community Coalition Concerned about Civilian Oversight of Police.

 www.geocities.com/CapitolHill/2381/Torontopoliceissues/occpsrulesofpractice.doc The general rules of practice for hearings and rulings conducted by the Ontario Civilian Commission on Police Services are available on this site, including terms and definitions as they apply to the rules.

CHAPTER TWO

CIVILIAN OVERSIGHT AND POLICE COMPLAINTS IN CANADA

LEARNING OBJECTIVES

1. Define civilian oversight of policing as it applies in Canada.
2. Identify the six components of the "cycle of police oversight."
3. Identify three qualities relevant to any system of civilian oversight of policing.
4. Identify several examples of civilian oversight from across Canada.
5. Identify key arguments for the introduction of civilian oversight of policing in Canada.
6. Define police complaints in Canada.
7. Identify several approaches for the handling of police complaints.
8. Describe the main features of the process for handling police complaints in various jurisdictions across Canada.
9. List the key categories of police complaints in Canada.

INTRODUCTION

This textbook has attempted to draw a distinction between overall schemes for civilian governance and police accountability in Canada, and the more specific applications of police oversight. In Chapter 1, the principles and concepts of governance and accountability were dealt with on a high level as they pertain to the relationship between policing and the public interest in Canada. Civilian governance and police accountability were seen to take shape within the Canadian context through a range of bodies that have differing levels of responsibility, but which are similar in that they hold police organizations to account for the propriety of their programs and activities.

In this chapter, we will look more closely at some of the precise oversight activities that are in existence in Canada. There will, again, be a concentration on the current oversight regime in existence in Ontario. However, other civilian oversight bodies across Canada will be reviewed in order to provide a relatively comprehensive picture. Because of the importance of policing in our society, and because it is imperative that the highest professional standards be in place for all police organizations, oversight agencies serve a vital purpose for the public good. Furthermore, this chapter will examine various approaches for dealing with police complaints in Canada.

ORIGIN OF CIVILIAN OVERSIGHT IN NORTH AMERICA

Intense controversy in the United States over excessive police action during the 1960s, as well as the influence of the civil rights and student protest movements in North America, resulted in steady and persistent demands for higher levels of police accountability. These demands were legitimate, especially in the face of clear instances of police misconduct and brutality. This development was reflected, on a somewhat less aggressive scale, in Canada. For example, the City of Metropolitan Toronto was a particular magnet for complaints about police behaviour. An example of this can be found in a series of raids on gay bathhouses in the late 1970s and early 1980s.

In February 1981, Metropolitan Toronto police officers conducted a series of raids on four gay bathhouses in the city and arrested more than 250 gay men, as well as some 20 others, who were charged as keepers of a common bawdy-house. This police action was extremely controversial, resulting in calls for greater external control over the police, and more significant oversight of police organizations. These particular police raids were followed by a demonstration of more than 3000 people, who blocked Yonge Street for several hours. This police action and the tactics involved were seen as being symptomatic of an approach to certain segments of the community that was not acceptable.

The formation of the Citizens' Independent Review of Police Activities (CIRPA) in Toronto also focused attention on the pressing need for police reform (McMahon and Ericson, 1984). Beyond the concerns of gay and lesbian groups, there was a growing demand for greater openness and accountability on the part of the police services. Citizens were seeking more participation across the range of policing activities and law enforcement approaches. Ethnic communities across Canada were also beginning to express concerns about police attitudes toward visible minorities and the quality of race relations within police organizations.

WHAT IS CIVILIAN OVERSIGHT OF POLICING?

Civilian oversight of policing refers to the actual mechanics of holding police accountable for their conduct. It refers to the entire system for ensuring that policing services are delivered in a manner that is conducive to the public good and in accordance with standards of justice that obtain in any given jurisdiction. Civilian oversight pertains significantly to those processes in place for dealing with public complaints about policing. In Chapter 3 we will look at the specifics of police discipline and the related topic of police ethics. However, in this chapter, we are concerned with the agencies, boards, and commissions that embody our notions of police accountability and oversight.

GENERAL FEATURES OF A CIVILIAN OVERSIGHT SYSTEM

Generally, any system of civilian oversight should strive to demonstrate the following qualities:

- Independence;
- Fairness; and
- Objectivity.

Beyond that, the process functions that should be included in any oversight system are as follows:

- Monitoring and review;
- Investigation;
- Adjudication;
- Resolution and penalty assessment;
- Appellate review; and
- Recommendation.

As part of a major review of policing that took place in Ontario under the auspices of the Ontario Ministry of the Solicitor General and Correctional Services in 1996, the following general observations were made with reference to the oversight of policing:

> Today, the need for an established and transparent system of oversight of police has been universally accepted by government, the police, and the communities they serve. It is recognized that the ability of the police to protect the community and to apprehend those who break the law relies, in large measure, on the trust and cooperation of the public. The police would be profoundly hindered in the performance of their duties without the willing support of the public.
>
> A competent civilian presence within such a system reinforces the fundamental principle that the extraordinary powers and authority of the police are a grant from the public, an essential condition of which is full and fair accountability to the public in their exercise. (p. 56)

In his detailed review of the relationship between the Special Investigations Unit and police services in Ontario, the Honourable George Adams (1998) notes that:

> Policing is the provision of an important public service. However, unlike most public service providers, the police are given extraordinary powers to detain civilians and, when reasonably necessary to prevent death or serious injury to themselves or civilians, to use lethal force. Therefore, the daily decisions of police officers may have a dramatic impact on the communities they serve as well as on their own lives. Any public service career is a demanding one, but given the nature of police work and the need to exercise related police powers responsibly, there are few public service careers more challenging. Public and police officer safety in a democratic society have led inevitably to issues of accountability. (p. 8)

It may, therefore, be useful to begin with a consideration of the cycle of police oversight. Figure 2.1, below, sets out the elements of this cycle.

FIGURE 2.1

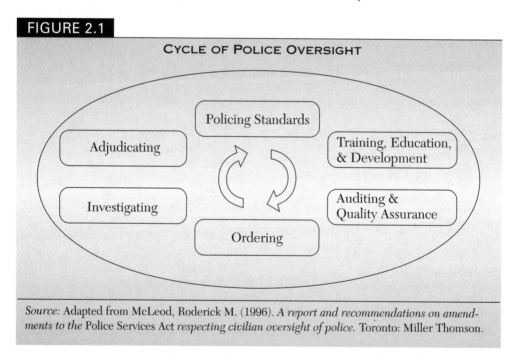

CYCLE OF POLICE OVERSIGHT

Source: Adapted from McLeod, Roderick M. (1996). *A report and recommendations on amendments to the* Police Services Act *respecting civilian oversight of police.* Toronto: Miller Thomson.

Any respectable system of police oversight should properly begin with detailed police standards. This implies an outline of expected levels of police activity, administration, and aptitude. Police standards would apply to such areas as:

- Dealing with the public;
- Arrest, search, and seizure;
- Handling of evidence;

- Response to calls for service;
- Investigations (criminal, traffic, and other);
- Interviewing witnesses and suspects;
- Police pursuits; and
- Use of force (non-lethal and lethal).

There could be any number of other areas where police standards might be in place to guide and direct appropriate action by police officers. The work of the Commission on Accreditation of Law Enforcement Agencies (CALEA) in the United States is an excellent example of a substantive effort at articulating police standards that are applicable in virtually every police service. CALEA has developed standards that address the following nine key law enforcement areas (1990):

1. Role, responsibilities, and relationships with other agencies.
2. Organization, management, and administration.
3. Personnel structure.
4. Personnel process.
5. Operations.
6. Operational support.
7. Traffic operations.
8. Prisoner and court-related activities.
9. Auxiliary and technical services.

In fact, several Canadian police organizations (e.g., Camrose (Alberta) Police Service, Edmonton Police Service, Lethbridge Police Service, Winnipeg Police Service, Niagara Regional Police Service, and Peel Regional Police Service) have adopted the CALEA standards as part of their drive for increased efficiency and effectiveness. Also, the recently implemented Adequacy and Effectiveness of Police Services Regulation (O.Reg.3/99) under the *Police Services Act* in Ontario is extremely helpful in understanding the full range of possible standards that can apply to professional police organizations. By establishing such standards for police activity, it becomes easier to determine if there are deficiencies that need to be addressed within any given police organization.

The first step for police organizations to take to ensure that their officers are functioning in a manner that is consistent with available policing standards involves the next phase of the cycle of oversight: ongoing and relevant police training, education, and development. There are several approaches to the design, delivery, and evaluation of quality police learning programs (Ontario. Ministry of the Solicitor General. Strategic Planning Committee on Police Training and Education, 1992; McKenna, 1998; McKenna 2000) but it is essential that any police learning curriculum be closely tied to the performance objectives officers are expected to achieve and consistent with existing standards. It is also important to recognize that since standards are open to change and revision, police learning programs must be flexible and adaptable to accommodate any modifications that may occur. This would be consistent with the concepts of organizational learning and continuous improvement that should animate any progressive police organization.

The next element in the cycle of police oversight is "auditing and quality assurance." This element relates to the formalized process of examining organizations against existing standards in order to discover if they are adhering to benchmarks and best practices. This should also be consistent with a continuous improvement model that sees value in providing the wherewithal for organizations to continually develop. However, it is essential that a process of review be conducted to ensure that the police organizations are indeed maintaining and observing standards, as well as conducting regular and consistent programs of police officer training, education, and development in a manner that will ensure the observance of policing standards.

The next phase in the cycle of oversight involves ordering, which speaks to the specific element of discipline within a police service. Clearly, as paramilitary organizations, police departments must be able to direct their employees to undertake certain activities within their ambit of responsibility and jurisdiction. As noted by Shearing (1992), there is an onus on police managers to ensure that order, or discipline, is maintained within the police service:

> The central feature of police management is the shaping of police conduct. Police managers are required to ensure that those under their supervision act in ways that promote the objectives of the police organization. They are required to create a particular organizational order; in other words, to guarantee a particular way of doing things. (p. 5)

This would include the ordering of the way things are done with respect to the "core services" of policing:

- Crime prevention;
- Law enforcement;
- Assistance to victims of crime;
- Public order maintenance; and
- Emergency response.

Next in the cycle of police oversight is the element of investigating, where it is necessary to actually examine, in some specific detail, the efforts of any particular police officer, or any police organization, within the context of the policing standards that have been approved within that jurisdiction. Rules and procedures for fair treatment must be in place to respect the rights of police officers, both as employees and as citizens.

Finally, the last phase in the cycle of police oversight deals with adjudicating. This pertains to the process of making appropriate judgments and includes recommendations for future behaviour within a police service. The process of adjudication, by definition, requires a considerable degree of judgment to be brought to bear on the merits of a particular case. Accordingly, a judicial officer is typically in an excellent position to provide a determination of the facts and assign responsibility. We will deal with the various approaches to police discipline in Chapter 3.

As is noted in McLeod's report and recommendations on civilian oversight in Ontario (1996):

> Civilian oversight at the Provincial and Local levels should not be the cause of FIDO (Forget It, Drive On). People in positions of authority in the Cycle of Oversight should have the respect and confidence of the whole public, including police officers and minority communities. The overseers should recognize the difficulties and dangers of police work and be champions of and advocates for good policing and the thousands of excellent people we have serving as police officers today. (p. 2)

The following section will review the key features of the civilian oversight systems in place in various jurisdictions across Canada. We will begin with an examination of the province of Ontario. Next, there will be a brief look at the federal level and the oversight of the Royal Canadian Mounted Police. Following this review, we will look at several provincial jurisdictions and their civilian oversight regimes. It should be noted that this treatment is current as of the date of publication, and is not intended to be exhaustive, but rather to give an overview of existing oversight structures in place in different areas across the country.

ONTARIO

REVIEW OF CIVILIAN OVERSIGHT OF POLICE IN ONTARIO

In 1996, then attorney general Charles Harnick announced that the government would be undertaking a comprehensive review of Ontario's system of civilian oversight of police. It was acknowledged that the existing system was confusing and a source of frustration for police officers and the public alike. With a view to creating a more effective and efficient civilian oversight system, the Ontario government authorized a review of the existing approach to civilian oversight and anticipated recommendations that would help to streamline the oversight process, eliminate any unnecessary duplication, and improve public accountability.

There were, in addition to chiefs of police, six civilian organizations that had some role in oversight, namely:

1. Office of the Police Complaints Commissioner;
2. Board of Inquiry;
3. Special Investigations Unit;
4. Ontario Civilian Commission on Police Services;
5. Police services boards; and
6. Policing Services Division of the Ministry of the Solicitor General and Correctional Services.

Approximately 86 full-time staff worked in the four civilian oversight agencies funded entirely by the province (i.e., the Office of the Police Complaints Commissioner, the Board of Inquiry, the Special Investigations Unit, and the Ontario Civilian Commission on Police Services). The total budgets for these organizations in 1996 amounted to more than $8.5 million.

This review was lead by Rod McLeod, a former assistant deputy attorney general, director of criminal law, and deputy solicitor general. McLeod's recommendations lead to the integration of the work done by the Office of the Police Complaints Commissioner and the Board of Inquiry into the mandate of the Ontario Civilian Commission on Police Services.

In Ontario, the current system of police oversight includes the following organizational elements, each responsible for various components of the system's overall effectiveness and efficiency:

• Chiefs of police and commissioner of the OPP;
• Police services boards;
• Ontario Civilian Commission on Police Services (including the previous roles of the Office of the Police Complaints Commissioner and the Board of Inquiry);
• Special Investigations Unit; and
• Ministry of the Solicitor General, Policing Services Division.

CHIEFS OF POLICE AND COMMISSIONER OF THE OPP

While chiefs of police in Ontario (including the commissioner of the Ontario Provincial Police) are not civilians, they do have an oversight role in that they are responsible under the *Police Services Act* for maintaining standards of performance and discipline within their respective forces. They have a duty to investigate incidents of wrongdoing, which duty is typically carried out in a delegated manner. The chief of police (or Commissioner) will determine, based on the results of an investigation, whether or not a form of misconduct has taken place. We will discuss disciplinary actions available to the chief of police in detail in Chapter 3.

POLICE SERVICES BOARDS

In Ontario, police services boards govern municipal police services, as discussed in Chapter 1, and they are generally responsible for the provision of adequate and effective policing in their municipal jurisdiction. They have an oversight function that includes holding misconduct hearings where the chief of police is the subject officer. Police services boards may also hear appeals by officers found guilty of misconduct following internal discipline hearings that have not resulted from a public complaint.

ONTARIO CIVILIAN COMMISSION ON POLICE SERVICES

As we have seen from our examination in Chapter 1, the Ontario Civilian Commission on Police Services (OCCPS) is an independent, quasi-judicial civilian agency that reports to the solicitor general. OCCPS was created by the *Police Services Act* and is the successor agency to the Ontario Police Commission (created in the early 1960s). OCCPS constitutes a broad enforcement authority for policing in Ontario and concerns itself with matters of adequacy and institutional performance. However, it also performs extremely important oversight functions. OCCPS may, at the request of the solicitor general, a municipal council, or of its own motion, conduct an inquiry into the conduct of any police officer or a member of a police services board. The commission has the power to impose penalties if it finds that an officer or member is not performing his or her duties in a satisfactory manner. Penalties that may be applied include dismissal, removal, or demotion. In performing its duties, the OCCPS has the powers of a commission under the *Public Inquiries Act*.

In addition to such adjudicative and regulatory functions, OCCPS is also the appellate tribunal for police officers found guilty following a disciplinary hearing. OCCPS currently has six employees and administers an annual budget of approximately $633 000.

THE SPECIAL INVESTIGATIONS UNIT

The Special Investigations Unit can trace its origins back to the hearings of the Ontario Race Relations and Policing Task Force that took place in 1988. During the course of hearings conducted as part of their mandate, Task Force members heard about concerns relating to the integrity of the process by which police conducted investigations involving other police officers or other police services. Many presenters questioned the objectivity of this approach and were particularly concerned about investigations involving the shooting of criminal suspects. As a result of these expressed concerns, the Task Force in its final report (1989) made a recommendation to the Ontario solicitor general that:

Credit: Special Investigations Unit

The new headquarters of the Special Investigations Unit.

...the Solicitor General create an investigative team to investigate police shootings in Ontario. That team should be comprised of homicide investigators chosen from various forces other than the force involved in the shooting, together with at least two civilian members drawn from government investigative agencies independent of the Ministry of the Solicitor General. When warranted, criminal charges should be laid within 30 days of commencing the investigation except [where] special circumstances justify extension. (p. 150)

As part of an overall revision of the policing framework in Ontario, the Special Investigations Unit (SIU) was created through provisions within the *Police Services Act*, which received royal assent on June 28, 1990. Part VII of the Act creating the SIU was proclaimed in force on August 8, 1990. As a result of a subsequent review of race relations in Ontario, conducted by Stephen Lewis, the SIU was made an arm's-length agency that reported to the Ontario Ministry of the Attorney General.

The SIU is a civilian agency in Ontario that is mandated with authority to investigate circumstances involving serious injury, including sexual assault, or death that may have resulted from criminal offences by police officers. Part VII of the *Police Services Act* creates the SIU and defines its powers. Figure 2.2 shows the current organizational structure of the SIU.

The SIU investigates occurrences throughout the province of Ontario that involve municipal, regional, and provincial police officers. The SIU director may, at her or his initiative, and shall, at the request of the solicitor general or the attorney general, cause an investigation to be conducted into the circumstances of serious injuries or deaths involving police officers.

FIGURE 2.2

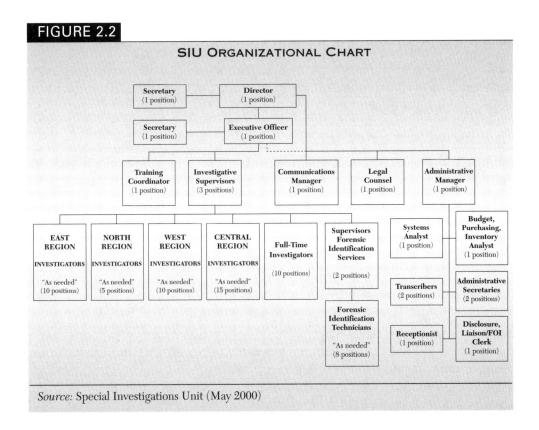

SIU ORGANIZATIONAL CHART

Source: Special Investigations Unit (May 2000)

DEFINITION OF "SERIOUS INJURY"

While the definition of "death" is non-controversial from the perspective of most people, "serious injury" has proven to be a concept that is open to considerable debate and, therefore, has required some degree of interpretation. When the SIU was beginning its operations, the first director, Mr. Justice John Osler, undertook consultations with the Ontario Ministry of the Solicitor General and the Ontario Association of Chiefs of Police to settle upon a shared understanding of this concept. This resulted in the following definition (Osler, 1999):

> "Serious injuries" shall include those that are likely to interfere with the health or comfort of the victim and are more than merely transient or trifling in nature and will include serious injury resulting from sexual assaults. "Serious injury" shall initially be presumed when the victim is admitted to hospital, suffers a fracture of a limb, rib or vertebrae [sic] or to the skull, suffers burns to a major portion of the body or loses any portion of the body or suffers loss of vision or hearing, or alleges sexual assault. Where a prolonged delay is likely before the seriousness of the injury can be assessed, the Unit should be notified so that it can monitor the situation and decide on the extent of its involvement. (p. 3)

INDEPENDENCE OF THE SIU

In order to underscore the independence of the SIU from any police service in the province, this agency reports to the Ontario attorney general. Beyond this reporting structure, however, the SIU conducts its investigations and makes its decisions independent of government.

DISCLOSURE OF INFORMATION

The SIU may decide to issue an initial press release once an incident it is involved with has occurred. However, during the course of an investigation, the SIU does not generally comment on or provide details about any particular case as it may place the integrity of the investigation and any potential subsequent prosecution in jeopardy. The SIU may make a public statement during an investigation where necessary to preserve the integrity of the investigation.

DECISIONS OF THE SIU DIRECTOR

Under section 113(7) of the *Police Services Act*, the director of the SIU holds exclusive authority to decide whether or not charges against a police officer are warranted. In arriving at this decision, the director will take into account all elements of an investigation and will arrive at his or her decision on the basis of "reasonable grounds." Where the director is of the opinion that there are reasonable grounds to do so, he or she causes a charge or charges to be laid against the officer or officers who were the subjects of the investigation. Once a charge is laid, the matter is referred to the Crown attorney for prosecution. Decisions of the SIU director are reported to the Ontario attorney general and the SIU may issue a press release on the director's decision, respecting the provisions of the *Freedom of Information and Protection of Privacy Act*.

THE ROLE OF THE SIU INVESTIGATOR

The provisions that are set out in the *Police Services Act* creating the SIU anticipate the need for skilled professionals who will be able to undertake investigations required to make determinations about police shootings and other events. These investigators are required to do the following:

1. Conduct objective, fair, thorough, and timely investigations into the issues addressed in the mandate governing the response of the Special Investigations Unit to Part VII of the *Police Services Act* by:
   - Receiving assignment and direction from Senior Special Investigations Unit Staff to conduct investigations.
   - Assessing the scope and determining the methodology needed to carry out an efficient investigation, including the need to evaluate the demand for specialized assistance and

support (e.g., obtaining identification or other forensic services and generally determining what evidence is required and who should be interviewed).
- Coordinating the list of people to be interviewed and interviewing both police and civilian witnesses to, or participants in, the incident being investigated.
- Gathering and analyzing evidence in accordance with the Prescribed Rules of Evidence and the law with respect to recognized investigative procedures and as directed by Operational Procedures of the Special Investigations Unit.
- Preparing comprehensive reports of investigations and, as may be required, making recommendations regarding action to be taken regarding the investigation.

2. As required or directed, provide assistance to Crown attorneys in the preparation of cases where charges are laid by:
- Obtaining additional evidence as may be required to support the charge in question.
- Preparing Crown briefs for presentation before the court.
- Providing all information obtained during the investigation the Crown attorney considers relevant to the charge.

3. Perform other duties relative to the investigative task, which include the ability to:
- Appear as a witness and give evidence during trials, coroner's inquests, or any other form of hearing.
- Attend courses, seminars, and training sessions related to the administrative and operational duties of the Special Investigations Unit.
- Demonstrate an understanding for the need to be sympathetic, tolerant, patient, and sensitive to the needs of all persons involved in the investigative process and to the public and its communities, in keeping with the mandate of the Special Investigations Unit.

The skills and knowledge required to perform the investigator's job at a full working level have been identified by the SIU as follows. Using a sound knowledge and understanding of relevant constitutional law, the *Criminal Code of Canada*, the *Canada Evidence Act*, the *Coroner's Act*, the *Police Services Act* of Ontario, and the mandate governing the response of the Special Investigations Unit, investigators must develop and demonstrate the ability to:

- Conduct comprehensive, impartial, diligent, and competent investigations.
- Plan the process of both long- and short-term investigations and initiatives.
- Gather relevant evidence and data and logically analyze them for their potential use.
- Impartially analyze the conduct and behaviour of persons involved in the investigative process.
- Recognize the importance of, and have the ability to gather details of importance to, the investigation.
- Critically examine suggestions and advice received during the investigative process.

SIU forensic identification team capturing digital images.

- Orally, and in writing, explain both the requirements and impact of the investigation or any particular part of it.
- Conduct in-depth interviews of both police and civilian witnesses to obtain all relevant information regarding the investigation.
- Participate in Special Investigations Unit outreach programs, which requires an understanding of police powers as they relate to the police and the public.

CONTROVERSY SURROUNDING THE SIU

During the 1998 review of the relationship between the Special Investigations Unit and police services in Ontario, the Honourable George Adams noted several points of controversy that existed at that time arising from different stakeholder groups and relating to the SIU and its operations. These included:

- *Community concerns*—community representatives expressed concerns about any delay in notification of the SIU and were disturbed that police association representatives and lawyers were notified well in advance of the SIU. Concerns were also raised about control of the incident crime scene, and the fact that witnesses are often identified, interviewed, and released prior to the arrival of SIU investigators. Also, there was alarm expressed over the fact that police officers were routinely claiming a constitutional right to silence and that this lack of immediate cooperation undermined the community's confidence in the police and the whole oversight process. Further, there were concerns registered around the failure of officers to complete their notes expeditiously following an incident and the perceived potential for collusion. Finally, there was an overriding concern that police officers and police representatives have failed to demonstrate their willingness to cooperate with the SIU, revealing a preference for police self-interest over against the public interest;

- *Police officer concerns*—officers expressed a degree of confusion over the SIU's legal jurisdiction and mandate. They suggested that this could, in part, explain delays in notification. It was pointed out that police officers in remote, or Northern, locations have a special challenge when it comes to preserving a crime scene and that the SIU was itself slow in getting investigators to the scene in such circumstances. Police officers also felt that SIU investigators did not have the training and expertise necessary to undertake complex investigations at the crime scenes to which their mandate applies. There was concern about the SIU's focus on possible criminal prosecutions and the unfair bias this carries with it for police officers involved. Police association representatives suggested that the real motivation behind the SIU's existence is a political one and places subject officers in a vulnerable position; and

- *Chiefs of police concerns*—Chiefs of police, and their representatives, cited their concerns over the lack of clear legal direction from the *Police Services Act* and the ambiguity of the Standard Operating Procedures (SOPs) for the SIU. They, too, noted the lack of investigator competence and resources. The chiefs of police were concerned about possible misuse of the media by the SIU and the overriding need to respect officers' legal rights and their health and safety concerns.

In March 1999, the executive of the Ontario Association of Chiefs of Police (OACP) issued its own definition of "serious injury" which did not have endorsement beyond the OACP. It is set out below:

"Serious Injury" shall mean:

1. Injuries that materially impair or interfere with the health of an individual, but does not include:
    a) fractures, cuts and burns that do not necessitate admission to acute medical care in hospital, or
    b) admissions to hospital for observation only.

2. Allegations, or real evidence, of sexual assault.

It is recognized that the OACP Executive's definition above would significantly narrow the number of incidents investigated by the SIU. The position of the SIU is that what is referred to as the "Osler definition" will remain in place until some process of public consultation has been set in motion to arrive at a clear consensus on any new definition.

Some police unions have historically been extremely vocal, and persistent, in their opposition to the SIU. This has been particularly true in Toronto, where the executive of the Toronto Police Association has, in the past, taken an aggressive stand against the agency. In May of 1997, the Toronto Police Association issued the following notice to its members (see Figure 2.3).

FIGURE 2.3

ATTENTION ALL MEMBERS

SPECIAL INVESTIGATIONS UNIT

Regardless of the Chief's recent Routine Orders and comments made by SIU Director Andre Marin in the Toronto Star, officers involved in SIU incidents <u>DO</u> have legal rights which *ARE* guaranteed by law.

Our Association role is to protect your legal rights by providing you with legal counsel.

Your role as an involved officer is to await your counsel's advice <u>BEFORE YOU SAY</u>

<u>OR WRITE ANYTHING.</u>

Until you speak to counsel, consider yourself to be an "involved officer" which provides you with ALL the fundamental rights guaranteed by the Canadian Charter of Rights and

Freedoms.

SAY NOTHING — WRITE NOTHING

Your counsel will advise you as to what steps should be taken.

CALL US FIRST

Source: Reprinted from Adams, G.W. (1998). *Consultation report of the Honourable George W. Adams, Q.C. to the Attorney General and Solicitor General concerning police cooperation with the Special Investigations Unit*. Toronto: George W. Adams, pp. 34–35.

As recently as August 2001, there were calls for the resignation of the SIU director from the presidents of the Police Association of Ontario and the Toronto Police Association. This particular form of police oversight seems to be difficult to accept for many police associations and the efforts at dialogue have not resulted in satisfactory solutions to the outstanding issues and concerns.

SIU OCCURRENCES

Table 2.1 provides a complete breakdown of SIU occurrences from its inception in 1990 until the year 2000.

TABLE 2.1

SIU OCCURRENCE CHART

Types of Offences	1990–1991[a]	1992	1993	1994	1995	1996	1997	1998	1999	2000
Firearm deaths	7	8	2	3	2	7	8	1	2	5
Firearm injuries	15	12	13	9	18	9	12	9	9	9
Custody deaths	6	14	14	11	20	27	11	21	20	17
Custody injuries	10	13	73	99	68	43	48	53	70	72
Vehicle deaths	6	5	11	12	6	7	8	10	14	7
Vehicle injuries	29	13	73	89	52	59	54	63	49	34
Sexual assaults	—	4	15	9	10	8	9	11	10	15
Total	**96**	**164**	**201**	**232**	**176**	**160**	**150**	**168**	**174**	**159**
Number of cases in which charges laid[b]	12	10	2	3	2	3	4	2 (5)	6 (6)	5 (10)

[a] The SIU began operations in September 1990.
[b] Number of officers charged shown in parentheses.

Source: Data provided by the SIU, December 31, 2000. Used with permission.

ONTARIO MINISTRY OF THE SOLICITOR GENERAL, POLICING SERVICES DIVISION

The overall vision for the ministry as part of its Business Plan for 2001–2002 is to implement innovative changes that will:

- Enhance front-line services;
- Increase accountability;
- Improve service quality; and
- Optimize cost-efficiency.

This division within the Ministry of the Solicitor General has the duty to administer the *Police Services Act*. It is responsible for inspecting municipal police services and police services boards and has recently introduced a system of quality assurance audits for police services. The existence of the Adequacy and Effectiveness of Police Services Regulation under the *Police Services Act* is important to note in this context as it fits into the whole cycle of police oversight cited above. The division prepares audit reports and promotes province-wide standards of policing through training and development.

Within the Policing Services Division there is a quality assurance unit that monitors and inspects police service management, administration, and operations, including the Canadian Police Information Centre (CPIC) system.

POLICE COMPLAINTS

An important part of the whole system of civilian oversight of policing deals with the handling of police complaints. These are complaints made by members of the public with regard to the actions, attitudes, behaviour, or performance of police officers. Police complaints may also extend to serious concerns about police performance at the organizational, or systemic, level. This section will look more closely at the manner in which police complaints are dealt with in various Canadian jurisdictions.

While it is essential that an effective system of police complaints be established and maintained, as Philips (1983) observes, the onus for holding and sustaining public trust rests ultimately with the police themselves:

> No complaints system can on its own convince the public that the police, with civility and without unnecessary force, are exercising their powers responsibly. The primary responsibility must remain that of the police, who have to achieve sensibly, responsibility to the public in general, accountability to the system in particular. This has important implications for police policies of recruitment and training. Moreover, if the complaints system is not solely to be seen as fulfilling a punitive role, necessary though that is, then the means must be found to seek and ensure improvement in police behaviour. (p. 113)

For a police complaints system to be worthwhile, police leaders and individual officers must be absolutely committed to its successful operation. Public trust is the priceless cornerstone upon which quality policing must rest. This point is made by Maloney (1975):

> An area of increasing public concern is the accountability of the police force to the society it is employed to serve and in particular the resolution of complaints by members of the public against individual officers. The reason for this concern is the growing appreciation that the effectiveness of any police department depends in the final analysis upon the degree of trust and cooperation it enjoys with the public. There is nothing more destructive of this relationship than a department unconcerned with complaints about its conduct or the service it provides. (p. 14)

In order to fashion a police complaints framework that serves the public interest, as well as the legitimate concerns of police officers, a degree of sensitivity is required in pursuing police complaints. Lewis (1991) addresses this need for moderation:

> One lesson which has been clear to the civilian administration of the Toronto complaints system is that restraint must be mixed with resolve. Resolve is necessary to confront inevitable police resistance and to match both police power and police perception of their power. Restraint is necessary to take account of the tumultuous effect of the imposition of significant review of police institutions. (p. 173)

HISTORY OF THE PUBLIC COMPLAINTS PROCESS IN ONTARIO

In the early 1970s, the Metropolitan Toronto Police developed an Internal Affairs Unit that was empowered to conduct internal investigations into the conduct of police officers. This was in response to the recommendations of the Knapp Commission in New York City and the controversies surrounding them. The motion picture *Serpico* is a dramatization of the events that led up to the calling of the Knapp Commission and was intended to address serious concerns about systemic police corruption within the New York City Police Department.

In 1983, the Metropolitan Toronto Police took part in a pilot project entitled Metropolitan Toronto Police Public Complaints Test Project. This lead to the enactment of the *Metropolitan Toronto Police Complaints Act*.

In 1990 the *Police Services Act* was introduced and all police services were required to form a Public Complaints Investigation Bureau. This legislation included guidelines for the conduct of investigations regarding public complaints. The entire regime was to be overseen by the Office of the Police Complaints Commissioner (PCC) and the PCC was to have authority to take control of police investigations, conduct investigations on its own, and hold hearings into allegations of police misconduct. In November 1997 the Ontario Legislature amended the *Police Services Act* and moved to:

* Terminate the position and office of the PCC;
* Transfer some of the authority of the PCC regarding police complaints to the OCCPS; and
* Simplify the handling of police complaints.

The amended legislation set a six-month time limit for the completion of investigations into police conduct complaints. Complaints must be in writing and signed by the complainant. The chief of police may dismiss complaints for reasons specified in the Act.

In Ontario, the police complaints process is now carried out under the auspices of the Ontario Civilian Commission on Police Services (OCCPS). In this capacity, the OCCPS has jurisdiction over:

* Sworn and civilian members of Ontario municipal police services and the OPP;
* Special constables;
* First Nations constables; and
* Auxiliary constables.

As discussed in Chapter 1, the OCCPS is guided by the *Police Services Act*. Powers of the commission include:

* Investigations with respect to the administration of municipal police matters;
* Inquiries with respect to crime and law enforcement matters;
* Inquiries about complaints regarding a police force's services and/or policies;

the conduct of an officer and the disposition of a complaint; and complaints made by a chief of police or a police services board;

- Reviews, at a complainant's request, into a chief's decision that a complaint is about the service or policies of a police force or about the conduct of an officer; that a complaint is vexatious or frivolous, made in bad faith, or unsubstantiated; that a complaint will not be dealt with because it was made more than six months after the facts on which it is based occurred; that the complainant was not directly affected by the service, policy, or conduct complained of; and that the misconduct or unsatisfactory work performance complained of is not of a serious nature;
- Hearing a police officer's appeals from decisions of a police chief, following an investigation where it was concluded that a police officer's conduct constituted misconduct or unsatisfactory work performance (section 64(7));
- Appeal hearings from decisions of a police board, following an investigation where it was concluded that a complaint about the conduct of a municipal chief or deputy chief of police is unsubstantiated (section 65(8)); and
- Hearings referred to a police board, following an investigation into misconduct or unsatisfactory work performance by a police chief or deputy chief (section 65(9)).

The OCCPS may also make recommendations about the services or policies of a police force by sending the recommendation to the solicitor general, the chief of police, or, in the case of a municipal police force, the police board.

CURRENT PUBLIC COMPLAINTS PROCESS IN ONTARIO

Two types of complainant are outlined in Part V, section 56(1) and (2) of the *Police Services Act*:

1. Public complaints by "any member of the public" about the policies of, or services provided by, a police service or the conduct of a police officer; and
2. Internal complaints made by a chief of police about the conduct of a police officer.

Complaints made by a chief of police may be processed under Part V of the *Police Services Act*.

DEFINITION OF A PUBLIC COMPLAINT

Section 57(1) of the *Police Services Act* defines who may make a public complaint by prohibiting third party complaints:

> A complainant may be made by a member of the public only if the complainant was directly affected by the policy, service or conduct that is the subject of the complaint.

Public complaints must be in writing and must be signed by the complainant. There is no statutory requirement that the complaint must be in a prescribed or standard format. Forms are available at every police station or from the OCCPS. Section 57(7) indicates that the following are *not* members of the public for the purposes of making a complaint:

(a) the Solicitor General;
(b) a member or employee of the Commission;
(c) a member of a police force if that police force or another member of that police force is the subject of the complaint;
(d) a member or employee of a board if the board is responsible for the police force, or a member of which is, the subject of a complaint; or
(e) a person selected by the council of a municipality to advise another municipality's board under subsection 6.1(2), if the board is responsible for the police force that is, or a member of which is, the subject the complaint; or
(f) a delegate to a community policing advisory committee if the [committee] advises the detachment commander of the OPP detachment that is, or a member of which is, the subject of the complaint.

Members of the public may make or withdraw a complaint at:

- The police station or detachment of the police service to which the complaint relates; or
- The commission.

Complainants may deliver a complaint or withdrawal personally or by an agent, by mail or facsimile. Complainants cannot use e-mail because the Act requires the complainant's signature on the complaint and a withdrawal. The commission must send a complaint or withdrawal of the complaint to the chief of police "forthwith." The commission does not investigate or resolve complaints.

The chief of police or the commissioner of the OPP must determine the nature of each complaint, whether it relates to the service or policies of the force or relates to the conduct of a police officer. The chief or the commissioner will ensure that conduct complaints are investigated, if not resolved or dismissed. Service or policy complaints are reviewed as appropriate by:

- An OPP detachment commander;
- A municipal police force chief; or
- The commissioner of the OPP if it is a provincial policy matter.

If the complainant disagrees with the initial classification of a complaint, he or she may request a review by the commission of that decision. The complainant has 30 days to request a review from the date of receiving the notice of the chief's or the commissioner's decision.

The chief of police or the commissioner may decide to dismiss a complaint because it:

- Was filed more than six months after the date the incident occurred;
- Is frivolous, vexatious or made in bad faith; or
- The complainant was not directly affected by the complaint.

Section 58 of the *Police Services Act* permits the chief of police to resolve a conduct complaint that is not of a serious nature, at any time, if both the complainant and the officer consent to the proposed resolution. This involves bringing the complainant and the officer together to discuss the complaint and to try to arrive at a mutually agreeable resolution. Statements made by the parties during an attempt at informal resolution are inadmissible at a civil proceeding, including disciplinary proceedings of the officer under Part V of the Act. Disciplinary actions pertaining to public complaints will be discussed in detail in Chapter 3. Table 2.2 shows the disposition of public complaints in Ontario in 1998.

TABLE 2.2

PUBLIC COMPLAINTS CASE DISPOSITION IN ONTARIO IN 1998

Category	Number[a]
Public complaints against officers in Ontario	2540
Files carried over from Police Complaints Commission	192
New reviews requested	472
Total reviews	664
Reviews completed	598 (90%)
Reviews withdrawn/abandoned	9 (1.5%)

[a]Figures in parentheses show the percentage of total reviews.

Source: Adapted from the Office of the Police Complaint Commissioner (2001).

ROYAL CANADIAN MOUNTED POLICE

COMMISSION FOR PUBLIC COMPLAINTS AGAINST THE RCMP

This body was created to provide an avenue for citizens to lodge complaints against members of the RCMP in the conduct of their duties. Part VII of the *RCMP Act* sets out the legislative framework for the commission. The following information outlines the vision, mission, mandate, and core values of the commission (Commission for Public Complaints Against the RCMP):

Vision

- Excellence in policing through accountability.

Mission

- To provide civilian oversight of RCMP members' conduct in performing their policing duties so as to hold the RCMP accountable to the public.

Mandate

- To receive complaints from the public about the conduct of RCMP members;
- To conduct reviews when complainants are not satisfied with the RCMP's disposition of their complaints;
- To hold hearings and carry out investigations; and
- To report findings and make recommendations.

Core Values

The following core values guide our work and reflect the work environment for which we strive:

- Independence
- Objectivity
- Fairness
- Timeliness
- Effective communication
- Excellence
- Respect
- Integrity
- Professionalism
- Teamwork

With respect to the process adhered to by the Commission for Public Complaints Against the RCMP, complaints may come to the Commission's attention by the following means:

- From members of the public directly to the RCMP;
- From members of the public to the Commission, or to provincial policing authorities; and
- Initiated by the Chair of the Commission.

Initially, all public complaints are investigated by the RCMP. Following this initial investigation, the RCMP commissioner reports the results to the complainant. If a complainant does not find the RCMP report satisfactory, the commission may be asked to undertake a review. The chair of the commission may take the following courses of action:

- Ask the RCMP to investigate further if there appears to be inadequacies in the investigation;
- Initiate her or his own investigation; or
- Hold a public hearing into the matter.

If the chair of the commission feels satisfied with the RCMP's disposition of a public complaint, she or he will report this finding to the complainant in writing, the RCMP members involved in the complaint, the RCMP commissioner, and the federal solicitor general. However, if the chair of the commission is not satisfied with the disposition of the matter, she or he will send an interim report to the RCMP commissioner and the solicitor general. The commissioner of the RCMP will inform the chair and the solicitor general, in writing, of any action that will be taken in order to respond to the findings and recommendations of the chair. This written response will include any rationale for a decision not to take any further action. Next, the chair of the commission will prepare a final report including any recommendations (as well as the text of the RCMP commissioner's response), which will be sent to the complainant, the RCMP members involved in the matter, the RCMP commissioner, and the solicitor general.

The chair of the commission is authorized to conduct hearings into specific complaints. This will normally happen only after information gathered by the RCMP or the commission has been carefully assessed. The chair of the commission has discretion to undertake a "public interest hearing" if such an inquiry is deemed to be worthwhile, even if the RCMP has conducted a prior investigation into the matter. The commission has received over 10 000 complaints since its inception in 1988. The RCMP accepts over 80 per cent of the commission's findings and recommendations.

Probably the most significant undertaking by the Commission for Public Complaints Against the RCMP to date is the APEC Hearing. The commission received a total of 52 complaints connected with events associated with the campus of the University of British Columbia during the Asia Pacific Economic Cooperation (APEC) conference. These complaints included concerns over excessive use of force by the police (deployment of pepper spray, police dogs, and physical constraints), oppressive conduct on the part of the RCMP, and violations of a constitutionally protected right to peaceful protest and demonstration. Consistent with its mandate, the commission instituted both a public interest investigation and hearing into these incidents. Specifically, the hearing was to inquire into the following:

- The events that took place during, or in connection with, demonstrations during the APEC conference held in Vancouver, British Columbia, between November 23 and 27, 1997, on or near the UBC campus and subsequently at the UBC and Richmond Detachments of the RCMP;

- Whether the conduct of members of the RCMP involved in the events was appropriate to the circumstances; and
- Whether the conduct of members of the RCMP involved in the events was consistent with respect for the Fundamental Freedoms guaranteed by section 2 of the *Canadian Charter of Rights and Freedoms*.

NEWFOUNDLAND

The Royal Newfoundland Constabulary Complaints Commission has jurisdiction over the Royal Newfoundland Constabulary (RNC), which patrols St. John's and surrounding areas, Corner Brook on the west coast of the island, and Labrador City. The RCMP patrols the rest of the province. The relevant legislation is the *Royal Newfoundland Constabulary Act, 1992* SN 1992 Chapter R-17 (amended: 1993 c.51, Consolidated Newfoundland Regulations 802/96 and 970/96). The functions of the commissioner and the commission are as follows:

- To receive and maintain a registry of complaints made by members of the public against police officers;
- To monitor the internal RNC investigation of such complaints and their disposition;
- To hear appeals against the decision of the Chief of Police subsequent to such internal investigation;
- To conduct an independent investigation of the circumstances giving rise to the complaints in respect of which appeals have been lodged;
- To effect a mutually agreed settlement among the parties;
- To refer the matter to an adjudicator for a public hearing when an agreed settlement is unattainable;
- [To] assume responsibility for the carriage of the case before the adjudicator; and
- [To] make recommendations to appropriate authorities respecting matters of public interest related to police services.

The commission received 64 public complaints in the period from April 1996 to March 1997 with the following disposition or conclusion, as shown in Table 2.3.

NEW BRUNSWICK

The New Brunswick Police Commission and the New Brunswick Complaints Commission have jurisdiction over police officers appointed pursuant to section 10, 11, or 17.3 or appointed by an interim policing authority, and over auxiliary police officers, but the commission does not have jurisdiction over members of the RCMP. The guiding legislation in this province is the *Police Act*, S.N.B. 1977, Chapter P-9.2.

TABLE 2.3

DISPOSITION OF COMPLAINTS FILED WITH THE ROYAL NEWFOUNDLAND CONSTABULARY COMPLAINTS COMMISSION, APRIL 1996 TO MARCH 1997

Category	Number	Percentage
Outside jurisdiction of the commission	4	6%
Withdrawn by complainant	12	19%
Informal resolution	3	5%
Insufficient evidence to substantiate a complaint	17	27%
Dismissed by the chief of police	9	14%
Pending (investigation ongoing)	19	29%
Total	64	100%

Notes: Four complaints resulted in discipline proceedings against the officer. Three cases were under appeal from a decision of the commission and/or adjudicator.

Source: Adapted from the Office of the Police Complaint Commissioner (2001).

The statutory duties and powers of the New Brunswick Police Commission are:

- The investigation and determination of complaints by any person about the conduct of a member of a municipal or regional police force;
- The investigation and determination of any matter relating to any aspect of policing in any area of the province either on its own motion or at the direction of the solicitor general;
- The determination of the adequacy of municipal, regional, and RCMP forces within the province.

The complaints registered with the New Brunswick Police Commisission from 1996 to 1998 are shown in Table 2.4. The disposition of those complaints is shown in Table 2.5.

NOVA SCOTIA

The Nova Scotia Police Commission and the Police Review Board have jurisdiction over the sworn members of the 17 municipal departments of the provincial police and special constables and by-law enforcement officers of Nova Scotia. The guiding legislation in this province is the *Police Act*, R.S.N.S., 1989, Chapter 348 as amended 1992, chap. 28, ss. 1-26; 1994-95, chap. 7, ss. 89-90, 150 and Regulations.

TABLE 2.4

COMPLAINTS REGISTERED WITH THE NEW BRUNSWICK POLICE COMMISSION, 1996 TO 1998

Complaint	1996–1997	1997–1998
Abuse of authority	38	24
Improper conduct	68	56
Neglect of duty	11	13
Other	14	8
Total	131	101

Source: Adapted from the Office of the Police Complaint Commissioner (2001).

TABLE 2.5

DISPOSITION OF COMPLAINTS FILED WITH THE NEW BRUNSWICK POLICE COMMISSION, 1996 TO 1998

Complaint Disposition	1996–1997	1997–1998
Founded	19	11
Outside jurisdiction	0	5
Pending (investigation ongoing)	1	1
Unfounded	53	63
Unsubstantiated	5	6
Withdrawn, discontinued, or closed	53	15
Total	131	101

Source: Adapted from the Office of the Police Complaint Commissioner (2001).

The Nova Scotia Police Commission was established in 1976 by proclamation of the *Police Act*. The commission reported to the attorney general and was responsible for improving municipal police forces and relations between the police and the public. In 1992 the commission was reorganized and re-oriented by legislative amendment. It now has responsibility for investigating matters relating to the conduct and performance of duties by police, the administration of municipal police forces, the system of policing in a municipality, and the police needs of a municipality.

The Nova Scotia Police Review Board was established in the mid-1980s by way of legislative amendments to the *Police Act*. The board became the adjudicating body for citizen complaints and appeals by police officers from internal discipline decisions by senior officers. The commission is responsible for investigating and negotiating a resolution to public complaints. The commission refers unresolved complaints to the board for a hearing. The chairman of the commission is also the registrar of the board. The commission provides administrative services to the board.

The duties and powers of the Nova Scotia Police Commission are as follows:

1. Consult and advise boards of police commissioners and other police authorities and chiefs of police on all matters relating to public complaints in accordance with the Act;
2. Conduct investigations and inquiries in accordance with the Act;
3. Provide investigative and administrative support to the Police Review Board;
4. Make recommendations with respect to amendments to the Act or the regulations or to any other enactment dealing with law enforcement;
5. On its own motion, or at the direction of the solicitor general, or at the request of a police board, inquire into
    *   the conduct and performance of any member of a municipal police force,
    *   the administration of any police force,
    *   the system of policing in any municipality, or
    *   the police needs of a municipality.
6. On the direction of the solicitor general, any matter relating to the extent, investigation or control of crime, and the enforcement of law.

The primary role of the commission is to investigate and conduct hearings into citizens' complaints alleging misconduct on the part of municipal police officers. The Commission's Police Review Board is also empowered to hear and determine appeals by police officers against disciplinary penalties or dismissals imposed by chiefs of police and boards of police commissioners. "Boards of police commissioners" refers to the municipal boards of police commissioners appointed under section 14 of the *Police Act* to administer the organization, budget, and policies of municipal police forces. What follows is a presentation of specific defaults alleged in public complaints against police officers (Table 2.6) and the dispositions of public complaints (Table 2.7).

QUEBEC

The Police Ethics Commissioner (Commissionaire à la deontologie policière) and the Quebec Police Complaints Commissioner have jurisdiction over the members the Sûreté du Québec, the Montreal Urban Community Police, or any other municipal police

TABLE 2.6

DEFAULTS ALLEGED IN PUBLIC COMPLAINTS LODGED WITH THE NOVA SCOTIA POLICE COMMISSION

Default Alleged	1996	1997	1998
Abuse of authority	100	112	87
Corrupt practice	0	0	2
Deceit	2	0	4
Discreditable conduct	79	110	140
Improper disclosure	4	3	6
Improper use of firearm	5	9	0
Insubordination	0	0	2
Neglect of duty	42	35	78
Failure to meet public expectation	5	2	6
Damage to property	3	1	3
Violation of *Canadian Human Rights Act*	7	1	1
Consumption of alcohol	0	0	1
Total	247	273	330

Source: Adapted from the Office of the Police Complaint Commissioner (2001).

TABLE 2.7

PUBLIC COMPLAINT DISPOSITIONS IN NOVA SCOTIA, 1997 TO 1998

Public Complaint Disposition	1997	1998
Founded	3	6
Informal resolution	20	35
Other[a]	18	23
Still under investigation[b]	25	21
Unfounded[c]	44	49
Withdrawn	27	19
Total	137	153

[a] Includes complaints filed beyond the eligible period where extensions were not granted; complaints where officer resigned from force; and criminally investigated complaints.
[b] Includes investigations at the department level or the commission level, and cases where a hearing into the merits of the complaint is pending.
[c] Includes complaints investigated and deemed unfounded at department level and not appealed by the complainant, or complaints deemed unfounded by the Police Review Board.

Source: Adapted from the Office of the Police Complaint Commissioner (2001).

department or special constable. The legislation that guides these functions is *An Act Respecting Police Organization* or the *Loi sur l'organisation policière* (L.R.Q., c. O-8.1).

The province of Quebec is unique in its approach to police complaints because it has required an alternative resolution of complaints since 1990. Also, the 1990 Act (*An Act Respecting Police Organization*) contained:

- A Code of Ethics for police officers;
- An independent commissioner of police ethics to ensure the protection of the rights of citizens and to ensure that complaints are treated with efficiency, justice, and fairness;
- An independent committee, the Comité de deontologie policière, to review the commissioner's decisions, on the request of a party, with authority to order an investigation or a new investigation or hold a hearing into police conduct; and
- A process by which the decisions of the committee may be appealed by a party to a court.

The statutory duties and powers of the commissioner are limited to complaints against members of the Sûreté du Québec, the Montreal Urban Community Police, and other municipal police departments and special constables.

CONCILIATION

Unless it is contrary to the public interest, as determined by the commissioner, every complaint must be first submitted to conciliation. The conciliation process is mandatory for the police officer involved. The complainant, however, may put forth reasons as to why her or his complaint should not be dealt with via the conciliation process. The complainant must do this within 30 days from the date on the commissioner's notice to the complainant.

INVESTIGATION

The ordering of an investigation is solely the responsibility of the commissioner. The commissioner may order an investigation when it is in the public interest to do so and when the complaint involves:

- Death or serious bodily harm;
- A situation where police officers in general will be discredited in the eyes of the public;
- Criminal offences; or
- Repeat offences or other serious matters.

The objective of an investigation is to ascertain whether there is sufficient evidence to bring the police officer before the Comité de deontologie policière. If the parties consent, however, the conciliatory process can resume at any time.

MANITOBA

The Law Enforcement Review Agency (LERA) is an independent, non-police agency established under *The Law Enforcement Review Act* in 1985 to investigate public complaints about police. LERA deals only with complaints about municipal police performance arising out of the execution of duties. It does not investigate criminal matters. Criminal matters are referred to the Crown Attorney's office. LERA is staffed by a Commissioner, a registrar and professional investigators.

The Act applies to any peace officer employed by a municipal police department in Manitoba, including police chiefs. It does not apply to members of the RCMP.

Complaints about members of the RCMP should be directed to the Commission for Public Complaints Against the RCMP, at www.cpc-cpp.gc.ca or by calling toll-free 1-800-665-6878. Complaints about RCMP members received by LERA will be forwarded.

LERA investigates a citizen's allegation that a municipal police officer has committed any of the following disciplinary defaults:

- Abuse of authority, including;
    - Making an arrest without reasonable or probable grounds
    - Using unnecessary violence or excessive force
    - Using oppressive or abusive conduct or language
    - Being discourteous or uncivil
    - Seeking improper pecuniary or personal advantage
    - Without authorization, serving or executing documents in a civil process
    - Discriminating on the basis of race, nationality, religion, colour, sex, marital status, physical or mental handicap, age, source of income, family status, political belief, or ethnic or national origin.
- Making a false statement, or destroying, concealing, or altering any official document or record.
- Improperly disclosing any information acquired as a member of the police department.
- Failing to exercise discretion or restraint in the use and care of firearms.
- Damaging property or failing to report the damage.
- Being present and failing to assist any person in circumstances where there is a clear danger to the safety of that person or the security of that person's property.
- Violating the privacy of any person within the meaning of *The Privacy Act*.

- Contravening *The Law Enforcement Review Act* or any other regulation under this Act, except where the Act of regulation provides a separate penalty for the contravention.
- Assisting any person in committing a disciplinary default, or counselling or procuring another person to commit a disciplinary default.

Disciplinary alternatives relating to this jurisdiction are dealt with in Chapter 3.

Third-party complaints may be made on behalf of other persons. The commissioner must, however, notify the affected person and obtain that person's consent before proceeding with an investigation into the complaint.

Tables 2.8, 2.9, 2.10, and 2.11 show, respectively, the disposition of complaints, investigations conducted, and complainant demographics in Manitoba from 1994 to 1998.

TABLE 2.8

DISPOSITION OF COMPLAINTS FILED WITH THE LAW ENFORCEMENT REVIEW AGENCY, 1994 TO 1998

Complaint disposition	1994	1995	1996	1997	1998
Resolved at intake or after preliminary investigation	123 (60%)	123 (54%)	164 (56%)	169 (56%)	182 (52%)
Full investigation	82 (40%)	105 (46%)	127 (44%)	134 (44%)	167 (48%)
Total	205	228	291	303	349

Note: Figures in parentheses show the percentage of total depositions.

Source: Adapted from the Office of the Police Complaint Commissioner (2001).

TABLE 2.9

INVESTIGATIONS CONDUCTED BY THE LAW ENFORCEMENT REVIEW AGENCY, 1994 TO 1998

	1994	1995	1996	1997	1998
Investigations completed and closed	78 (62%)	70 (43%)	103 (48%)	59 (32%)	220 (59%)
Investigations carried over on Dec. 31, 1998	47 (38%)	94 (57%)	114 (52%)	126 (68%)	150 (41%)
Total	125	164	217	185	370

Note: Figures in parentheses show the percentage of total investigations conducted.

Source: Adapted from the Office of the Police Complaint Commissioner (2001).

TABLE 2.10

COMPLAINANT DEMOGRAPHICS IN MANITOBA, BY SEX

Sex	1994	1995	1996	1997	1998
Male	53 (65%)	77 (73%)	99 (78%)	104 (78%)	109 (65%)
Female	29 (35%)	28 (27%)	28 (22%)	30 (22%)	58 (35%)
Total	82	105	127	134	167

Note: Figures in parentheses show the percentage of complainants.

Source: Adapted from the Office of the Police Complaint Commissioner (2001).

TABLE 2.11

COMPLAINANT DEMOGRAPHICS IN MANITOBA, BY AGE

Age	1994	1995	1996	1997	1998
Over 50	8 (10%)	9 (9%)	11 (9%)	13 (10%)	19 (11%)
40–49	17 (21%)	13 (12%)	15 (12%)	21 (15%)	36 (22%)
30–39	17 (21%)	26 (25%)	35 (27%)	33 (25%)	44 (26%)
18–29	25 (30%)	32 (31%)	44 (35%)	35 (26%)	41 (25%)
Youths under 18	2 (2%)	11 (10%)	10 (8%)	13 (10%)	12 (7%)
Unknown	13 (16%)	14 (13%)	12 (9%)	19 (14%)	15 (9%)
Total	82	105	127	134	167

Note: Figures in parentheses show the percentage of complainants.

Source: Adapted from the Office of the Police Complaint Commissioner (2001).

The LERA's annual report for 1998 also contains comprehensive statistics for 1994 to 1998 on the following:

1. Location of incidents that gave rise to a complaint;
2. Referrals to Crown Counsel for criminal investigation;
3. Details about allegations of abuse of authority that specify the number of incidents alleging:
   - Injuries from use of force;
   - Misuse of pepper spray;
   - Misuse of handcuffs.

SASKATCHEWAN

The responsible organization is the Saskatchewan Police Complaints Investigator and it has jurisdiction over the sworn members of the 17 municipal police services and designated special constables operating in Saskatchewan. The legislation that guides this office is the *Saskatchewan Police Act*, 1990, R.S.S., 1990-91, c. P-15.01, Part IV, and the Municipal Police Discipline Regulations, 1991. Section 39(1) of the *Police Act* provides that:

> Where the Investigator receives a public complaint pursuant to section 38 the Investigator shall:
>
> - Record the complaint received;
> - Establish and maintain a record of all public complaints received by police services and their dispositions;
> - Inform, advise and assist complainants;
> - Advise and assist the chiefs and boards, the hearing officer and the commission with respect to the handling of public complaints;
> - Monitor the handling of public complaints and ensure that public complaints are handled in a manner consistent with the public interest;
> - Inspect annually, or at those times directed by the minister, the records, operations and systems of administration for the handling of public complaints by police services.

The investigator's powers relate exclusively to public complaints, not internal discipline, or service, or policy matters.

The Act also specifies three processes to deal with issues involving police conduct in Part IV:

- The public complaint process;
- The internal discipline process; and
- The non-disciplinary process.

The director of the Saskatchewan Police Complaints Investigator's office conducts external investigations. The director conducts approximately 18 investigations of public complaints per year. This office opened 182 complaint files between April 1, 1996, and March 31, 1997, and 132 public complaint files between April 1, 1997, and March 31, 1998. The director handles all public complaints for all municipal police services that have no internal investigator. The two largest departments, Regina and Saskatoon, each have an internal investigator assigned to investigate public complaints and internal discipline matters. The director also investigates particularly sensitive public complaints and those that require an independent investigation for some other reason. The findings of the Saskatchewan Police Complaints Investigator from 1996 to 1998 are shown in Table 2.12.

TABLE 2.12

COMPLAINT FINDINGS OF THE OFFICE OF THE SASKATCHEWAN POLICE COMPLAINTS INVESTIGATOR, 1996 TO 1998

Finding	1996–97	1997–98
Substantiated	49 (27%)	34 (24%)
Unsubstantiated	2 (1%)	5 (4%)
Unfounded	101 (56%)	81 (58%)
Withdrawn/Other	30 (16%)	18 (13%)
Not completed	0	2 (1%)
Total	182	140[a]

Note: Figures in parentheses show the percentage of complaint findings.

[a]Of the 132 complaints filed in 1997–98, eight were multiple complaints.

Source: Adapted from the Office of the Police Complaint Commissioner (2001).

DEFINITION OF COMPLAINT FINDINGS

The four categories of complaint findings are defined as follows:

- Substantiated—supported by the evidence on investigation
- Unsubstantiated—allegation cannot be proved or disproved
- Unfounded—allegation unsupported by the evidence
- Withdrawn/Other—includes informal resolutions, and abandoned and withdrawn complaints

The types of complaints lodged with the Saskatchewan Police Complaints Investigator are shown in Table 2.13.

ALBERTA

In Alberta, there are currently eight police commissions in place in the following cities: Calgary, Camrose, Coaldale, Edmonton, Lacombe, Lethbridge, Medicine Hat, and Taber.

LAW ENFORCEMENT REVIEW BOARD

This is an independent, quasi-judicial body established under the Alberta *Police Act* in 1973. Its principal objective is to provide an independent and impartial review

TABLE 2.13

COMPLAINTS LODGED WITH THE OFFICE OF THE SASKATCHEWAN POLICE COMPLAINTS INVESTIGATOR, 1996 TO 1998

Type of Complaint	1996–97	1997–98
Discreditable conduct	15	10
Neglect of duty	40	31
Insubordination	0	0
Improper disclosure of information	3	4
Corrupt practice	0	0
Abuse of authority	100	79
Improper use of firearms	0	0
Damage to police property	0	0
Improper wearing of uniform/personal appearance	0	0
Misuse of alcohol/drugs	0	0
Criminal conduct	2	2
Other	22	12
Undefined[a]	0	2
Total	182	140

[a]These complaints had not yet been categorized at the time of publication.

Source: Adapted from the Office of the Police Complaint Commissioner (2001).

into public complaints and for appeals by police officers as a result of disciplinary action by a police chief.

The main activity of the board is to hear appeals from citizens who have complained about a police officer's actions and who are not satisfied with the disposition of their complaint. Police officers subject to discipline from a complaint investigation who are aggrieved with the decision of the chief of police may also appeal to the Law Enforcement Review Board (LERB). The LERB provides a forum for both citizens and police officers independent of the police service involved.

Sworn members of the eight municipal police services and designated special constables operating in Alberta fall under the auspices of the Law Enforcement Review Board. The commissions and the LERB are not responsible for complaints concerning members of the RCMP. The significant legislation in this context is the Alberta *Police Act*, R.S.A. CP-12.01 1988, Parts 2, 3, and 5 and Police Service Regulation 356/90.

The *Police Act* in Alberta provides civilian oversight for municipal police conduct through the police commissions. These commissions are to generally oversee the police service, and their mandate includes funding, policies, and procedures, and the staffing of the service. The commissions or their delegates (the complaints monitor of each commission) review and comment on police service complaint investigations as to their:

- Adequacy;
- Thoroughness; and
- Fairness.

The Calgary and Edmonton Police Commissions have a complaints monitor, while the other commissions monitor public complaints according to their own practice. The commissions have eight functions within the oversight process:

1. Receive, review, and decide the outcome of complaints against the chief of police.
2. Audit the complaint process by reviewing public complaints about police officers. This includes reviews of complaint investigations and dispositions.
3. Report to the chair of the LERB on the status and disposition of all public complaints about the police service or individual officers.
4. Conduct appeals by citizens from the chief's decisions about police service or policy complaints. The chief may refer a citizen's service or policy complaint to the commission for disposition.
5. Inquire into matters respecting the police service or the actions of any police officer or other person employed by the police service (i.e., a civilian member).
6. Establish policies for efficient, effective policing.
7. Grant time limits under section 7 of the Police Service Regulation for the charging of an officer with a disciplinary offence, or the holding of a disciplinary hearing into an offence.
8. Review and confirm a chief's decision to "relieve from duty without pay any police officer whom the chief [or a senior officer] on reasonable grounds suspects has committed a disciplinary offence."

CALGARY POLICE COMMISSION

The Calgary Police Commission was described briefly in Chapter 1. With regard to its specific responsibilities in the area of public complaints, the following information is useful.

Under the *Police Act*, the responsibility for investigation of complaints against the police generally and against specific officers lies with the Chief of Police. The commission is the civilian body which is empowered to oversee the complaints process, receive complaints against the Chief of Police, and act as the appeal body for complaints against the police service as a whole.

CITIZEN COMPLAINTS MONITOR

The functions of the Citizens Complaints Monitor are as follows:

- Provides an independent review of the citizen complaints process of the CPS;
- Reviews the police service files of all public complaints to ensure investigations are appropriate, fair and thorough;
- Reports his or her findings directly to the commission;
- Makes public presentations to interested groups concerning the complaint process; and
- Receives complaints from the public.

BRITISH COLUMBIA

The British Columbia Office of the Police Complaint Commissioner is an independent agency established under the *Police Act*. This office is responsible for monitoring complaints against municipal police to ensure they are handled fairly and impartially. The Police Complaint Commissioner is an Officer of the Legislature. The office is completely independent from any police department or government ministry and reports directly to the Legislature. It came into being as a result of amendments to the British Columbia *Police Act*, proclaimed July 1, 1998. In July 1999, the *Police Act* was further amended to make modifications to the process whereby adjudicators for public hearings were appointed.

Many of the changes to the *Police Act* in British Columbia were brought about through the recommendations made by Mr. Justice Wallace T. Oppal, whose Policing in British Columbia Commission of Inquiry in 1994 examined, among other things, matters pertaining to civilian governance and police complaints.

Following a process of consultation with the 12 municipal police departments under its jurisdiction, the Office of the Police Complaint Commissioner released a set of guidelines, practice directives, and policies designed to assist in the process of interpreting the *Police Act* as it pertains to dealing with complaints.

Between the period of July 1, 1998, and July 31, 1999, the Office of the Police Complaint Commissioner concluded 214 files. Of that number, 202 files were identified as "public trust" complaint files, 10 were viewed a "service or policy" files, and 2 were characterized as "internal discipline." The "public trust" files were dealt with as shown in Table 2.14.

TABLE 2.14

DISPOSITION OF PUBLIC TRUST COMPLAINTS FILED WITH THE BRITISH COLUMBIA OFFICE OF THE POLICE COMPLAINT COMMISSIONER, 1998 TO 1999

Complaint Disposition	Number	Percentage
Abandoned	7	4%
Withdrawn	6	3%
Informally resolved	39	19%
Summarily dismissed	131	65%
Substantiated	19	9%
Total	202	100%

Source: Adapted from the Office of the Police Complaint Commissioner (2001).

CONCLUSION

This chapter has provided some further focus on civilian oversight of policing as it has evolved in Canada. Our concentration has been on the province of Ontario, however, we have considered other jurisdictions in this review. There is much more detail available on the specific civilian oversight bodies that are in place. Their mandates and functions are frequently under review and assessment; therefore, it is important to keep abreast of developments that may impact upon the operation of any of these agencies.

We have also looked at the whole area of police complaints as an expression of civilian oversight. The capacity of individual citizens to initiate complaints against police officers, or police organizations, is certainly a hallmark of an effective system of police oversight. We have paid some attention to the process and practice of police complaints across Canada, again, with a particular emphasis on the processes and procedures in place in Ontario.

QUESTIONS FOR CONSIDERATION AND DISCUSSION

1. What structure of civilian oversight best ensures effective and efficient public accountability of police organizations?
2. How could police oversight processes be streamlined in order to reduce delay and still ensure procedural fairness for complainants, subject officers, and their police service?
3. Are informal dispute resolution techniques valuable in speeding up the decision-making process and reducing costs associated with public complaints?

4. What are the appropriate accountability relationships between governments and civilian oversight organizations?
5. What oversight matters are of a purely local concern and which matters should be dealt with on a provincial or national basis?
6. What police conduct should be subject to civilian oversight?
7. Discuss the impact of the *Canadian Charter of Rights and Freedoms* on the issue of subject officers providing statements to civilian oversight bodies.
8. In Ontario, under the *Police Services Act*, what constitutes a chief's complaint?
9. How does one make a determination about the nature of a public complaint as to whether or not it is frivolous or vexatious?
10. What are a chief of police's obligations with regard to external investigations in Ontario?
11. In Ontario, when is the suspension of a police officer necessary? What are the key relevant issues?
12. What is the impact of an unsatisfactory work performance policy on an offence such as neglect of duty?

RELATED ACTIVITIES

1. Review the "Record of Proceedings" for the 6th Annual Canadian Association for Civilian Oversight of Law Enforcement conference held September 20–23, 2000, in Winnipeg, Manitoba, and consider some of the areas of concentration during this conference including:

    - Role of the media in affecting police conduct;
    - Affecting police conduct through ethics and training;
    - Affecting police conduct through informal resolution; and
    - Affecting police conduct through civilian oversight and self-management.

2. Select a civilian oversight body and prepare an organizational outline of that organization and its mission and mandate. Review any annual reports or newsletters prepared by the body and consult its website (if available) for additional information.
3. Review individual cases prepared by the Ontario Civilian Commission on Police Services that deal with the topics covered in this chapter.
4. Approach an individual police service in your jurisdiction and ask for information on handling public complaints. Look at statistical data and any procedural manuals that might be available as well as brochures and public information on the complaints process. Does the department demonstrate the features of an effective complaints system?
5. Examine media coverage of a death or serious injury involving a police service in Ontario where the Special Investigations Unit (SIU) has been called in to

investigate. How was the matter handled by the police service, the police association, the SIU, and the media? What public reactions occurred?

REFERENCES

Adams, G.W. (1978). *Grievance arbitration cases: a study of the concepts of industrial discipline and their results*. Kingston, Ont.: Industrial Relations Centre, Queen's University.

Adams, G.W. (1998). *Consultation report of the Honourable George W. Adams, Q.C. to the Attorney General and Solicitor General concerning police cooperation with the Special Investigations Unit*. Toronto: George W. Adams.

Australia. Law Reform Commission (1975). *Law Reform Commission report no. 1: complaints against police*. Canberra: Australian Government Publishing Service.

Barton, P. (1970). "Civilian review boards and the handling of complaints against the police." *University of Toronto Law Journal*, Vol. 20, pp. 448–69.

Bayley, D.H. (1983). "Accountability and control of police: some lessons for Britain." In Bennett, T. (ed.) *The future of policing: papers presented to 15th Cropwood Round-Table Conference, December 1982*. Cambridge: Institute of Criminology, University of Cambridge.

Office of the Police Complaint Commissioner (2001). British Columbia Office of the Police Complaint Commissioner website. [Cited November 23, 2001.] <www.opcc.bc.ca>.

Brown, D. (1985). "Civilian review of complaints against the police: a survey of the U.S. literature." In Heal, R. Tarling and J. Burrows (eds.) *Policing today*. London: HMSO.

Carter, G.E., Cardinal (1979). *Report to the civic authority of Metropolitan Toronto and its citizens*. Toronto: Office of the Cardinal.

Commission on Accreditation for Law Enforcement Agencies, (1990–). *Standards for law enforcement agencies: the standards manual of the Law Enforcement Agency Accreditation Program*. Fairfax, Virginia: The Commission.

Commission for Public Complaints Against the RCMP. Commission for Public Complaints Against the RCMP website. [Cited November 20, 2001.] <www.cpc-cpp.gc.ca>.

Goldsmith, Andrew J. (1988). "New directions in police complaints procedures: some conceptual and comparative departures." *Police Studies*, Vol. 11, pp. 60–71.

Goldsmith, Andrew J. (ed.) (1991). *Complaints against the police: the trend to external review*. Oxford: Clarendon Press.

Goldsmith, Andrew J. (1991). "External review and self-regulation: police accountability and the dialectic of complaints procedures." In Goldsmith, Andrew J. (ed.) *Complaints against the police: the trend to external review*. Oxford: Clarendon Press.

Grant, A. (1975). "The control of police behaviour." In Tarnopolsky, Walter S. (ed.) *Some civil liberties issues in the seventies*. Toronto: Osgoode Hall Law School, York University.

Landau, T. (1994). *Public complaints against the police: the view from complainants*. Toronto: Centre of Criminology, University of Toronto.

Law Enforcement Review Agency (2000). "What do we investigate?" [online]. [Cited November 20, 2001.] <http://www.gov.mb.ca/justice/lera/process/process.html>.

Lewis, Clare E. (1991). "Police complaints in Metropolitan Toronto: perspectives of the public complaints commissioner." In Goldsmith, Andrew J. (ed.) *Complaints against the police: the trend to external review*. Oxford: Clarendon Press.

Lewis, C.E., S.B. Linden and J. Keene (1986). "Public complaints against police in Metropolitan Toronto: the history and operation of the office of the public complaints commissioner." *Criminal Law Quarterly*, Vol. 29, pp. 115–144.

Maloney, A. (1975). *Report: the Metropolitan Toronto review of citizen-police complaint procedure*. Toronto: Metropolitan Toronto Board of Commissioners of Police.

McKenna, Paul F. (1998). *Foundations of policing in Canada*. Scarborough, Ont.: Prentice Hall Canada.

McKenna, Paul F. (2000). *Foundations of community policing in Canada*. Scarborough, Ont.: Prentice Hall Allyn and Bacon Canada.

McLeod, Roderick M. (1996). *A report and recommendations on amendments to the* Police Services Act *respecting civilian oversight of police*. Toronto: Miller Thomson.

McMahon, Maeve W. and Richard V. Ericson (1984). *Policing reform: a study of the reform process and police institution in Toronto*. Toronto: Centre of Criminology, University of Toronto.

McMahon, Maeve W. (1988). "Police accountability: the situation of complaints in Toronto." *Contemporary Crises*, Vol. 12, pp. 301–327.

New York. Commission to Investigate Allegations of Police Corruption and the City's Anti-Corruption Procedures (1972). *Commission report (with summary and principal recommendations, issued August 3, 1972)*. New York: George Braziller. (Whitman Knapp, Chairman.)

Ontario Association of Chiefs of Police (1999). Special Investigations Unit website. [Cited November 20, 2001.] <http://www.siu.on.ca/pol-act.htm>.

Ontario. Ministry of the Solicitor General. Strategic Planning Committee on Police Training and Education (1992). *A police learning system for Ontario: final report and recommendations*. Toronto: The Ministry.

Ontario. Ministry of the Solicitor General and Correctional Services (1996). *Policing Ontario: building for the future*. Toronto: The Ministry.

Ontario. Race Relations and Policing Task Force (1989). *The report of the Race Relations and Policing Task Force*. Toronto: Ministry of the Solicitor General.

Ontario Civilian Commission on Police Services (1992). *Report of an inquiry into administration of internal investigations by the Metropolitan Toronto Police Force*. Toronto: The Commission.

Oppal, The Honourable Wallace T. (1994). *Closing the gap: policing and the community: the report, volume 1*. [Victoria, B.C.]: Policing in British Columbia Commission of Inquiry.

Osler, John (1999). *SIU Hotline* (Spring), Vol. 3, no. 1. Official newsletter of the Special Investigations Unit.

Philips, Cyril (1983). "The police complaints system in England and Wales." In Bennett, T. (ed.) *The future of policing: papers presented to the 15th Cropwood Round-Table Conference December 1982*. Cambridge: Institute of Criminology, University of Cambridge.

Russell, K. (1976). *Complaints against the police: a sociological view*. Leicester: Milltak.

Scarman, L. (1982). *The Scarman report: the Brixton disorders 10-12 April 1981*. Harmondsworth: Penguin.

Shearing, Clifford D. (1990). *Post-complaint management: the impact of complaint procedures on police discipline*. Ottawa: Royal Canadian Mounted Police External Review Committee. (Discussion paper; no. 4.)

Shearing, Clifford D. (1992). *Reflection on police management practices*. Ottawa: Minister of Supply and Services Canada. (Discussion paper series: no. 12.)

Stenning, Philip C. (2000). "Evaluating police complaints legislation: a suggested framework." Presentation to the 6th Annual CACOLE conference, September 20–23, 2001, Winnipeg, Manitoba.

Terrill, R. (1980). "Complaint procedures against police: the movement for change in England, Canada and Australia." *Police Studies*, Vol. 3, pp. 37–46.

Terrill, R. (1982). "Complaint procedures: variations on the theme of civilian participation." *Journal of Police Science and Administration*, Vol. 10, pp. 398–406.

Watt, Susan A. (1991). "The future of civilian oversight of policing." 33 *Canadian Journal of Criminology*, 347.

Weiler, P.A. (1969). "Who shall watch the watchmen? Reflections on some recent literature about the police." *Criminal Law Quarterly*, Vol. 11, p. 420.

WEBLINKS

 www.gov.mb.ca/justice/lera Although police officers generally perform their duties according to the law and with consideration for the public good, citizens sometimes feel they have been treated unjustly. These complaints are registered, investigated, and resolved according to the procedures established under the Law Enforcement Review Act.

 www.opcc.bc.ca/canadian.htm The website of the British Columbia Office of the Police Complaint Commissioner, an independent agency established under the *Police Act*, provides information for citizens on how to make a complaint against the police in British Columbia, and explains the complaint resolution process.

 www.walnet.org/csis/reports/junger_inquiry/s_watt.html This website offers a case study by Susan Watt (Police Complaints Commissioner of Ontario) on the future of civilian oversight of policing in Toronto.

 www.ombudsman.dnd.ca/speeches/spch22_e.asp This website offers a speech entitled *Civilian Oversight: Myth or Reality* given by André Marin, Ombudsman for the Department of National Defence and the Canadian Forces.

 www.opcc.bc.ca/CACOLE%20Papers/Stenning.html Philip C. Stenning, Associate Professor in the University of Toronto's Centre of Criminology, provides a detailed discussion of a suggested framework for evaluating police complaints legislation.

www.siu.on.ca The Special Investigations Unit of Ontario website explains its role as the civilian agency dealing with situations that may have resulted from criminal offences committed by police officers.

CHAPTER THREE

POLICE DISCIPLINE AND ETHICS

LEARNING OBJECTIVES

1. Identify several approaches to police discipline in Canada.
2. List the common offences relevant to police codes of conduct in Canada.
3. Define police ethics as it applies within a Canadian context.
4. Identify the elements of the model of police ethics developed by the Canadian Association of Chiefs of Police.

INTRODUCTION

This chapter will examine two closely related police topics: discipline and ethics. The concept of police discipline is unique because it relates to a public service that observes rules and regulations that are more closely akin to a military model where command and control principles have importance. Unlike other professional organizations that have some form of disciplinary regime, police departments continue to bind their officers by "orders" that limit or guide their range of functions or operations in a significant manner.

Ethics, on the other hand, refers to a more abstract understanding of the limits of appropriate and professional behaviour, and is typically guided by a number of specific principles. Unlike precise codes of conduct that enumerate particular actions that police officers must adhere to, ethical standards of policing are normally more focused on ideal models of behaviour and being. Ethics is concerned with considerations of character and integrity.

POLICE DISCIPLINE

For decades police discipline has been something that the public has known little, or nothing, about. When officers breached an existing code of conduct, they would receive discipline from their superior officers, and the matter was something that would rarely be publicized. Until only recently, police organizations would not allow any degree of control of their discipline systems to move beyond the police hierarchy. Police associations and unions remain particularly opposed to external control and have invested significant energy and financial resources in resisting the growth of forms of police discipline and civilian oversight that they view as intrusive. As Lewis (1991) observes:

> Police organizations are very hostile to efforts to increase their public accountability through civilian incursion into their discipline systems. While police in democratic societies are subject to the rule of law and state allegiance both to legal constraints on their authority and to their obligation to account to civilian masters, they also operate organizationally by much more informal rules understood within the institution as more reflective and supportive of police attitudes and values. (p. 161)

The student should be conscious of the vital importance of the question: *Who will guard the guardians?* It was certainly a central question for philosophers, as Plato outlined in his *Republic*. But it remains a question that citizens and police executives must continue to ask as we continue to witness the growth of police organizations as agencies of public safety and control.

It is clear that guidelines need to be established to control the behaviour of police personnel (both civilian and uniformed) in their official capacities. Supervision of individual officers will be required but in addition there will be a need for regular inspections and a program of internal affairs to probe more deeply for any officers who may be willing to violate the established organizational parameters. The following is taken from the U.S. Commission on Accreditation for Law Enforcement Agencies (CALEA) standard on discipline procedures (1994):

CALEA Disciplinary Procedures

Standard 26.1.4

A written directive establishes a disciplinary system, to include:

a. procedures and criteria for rewarding employees;
b. procedures and criteria for using training as a function of discipline;
c. procedures and criteria for using counseling as a function of discipline; and
d. procedures and criteria for taking punitive actions in the interest of discipline.

The internal, or "closed," nature of police discipline meant that the public was never really aware of the nature or extent of police misconduct in any systematic way. On the other hand, it also meant that police officers did not always have an avenue of

Credit: Mike Weaver, Media Relations, Kingston Police

Police discipline is a reflection of police power.

public recourse for any unfair or arbitrary application of police discipline. Because police supervisors held sway over the working conditions, the promotional opportunities, and the operational deployment of their officers, it was entirely possible for officers to suffer from these arrangements in ways that might have been capricious or arbitrary. Bayley (1983, p. 154) provides some clear insight into the nature of internal controls within police departments. Informal mechanisms have always been in existence to control and constrain individual police behaviour, though not always in a positive or enlightened manner. From an American perspective, Sheehan and Cordner (1995) offer the following comments:

> Traditionally, discipline in law enforcement agencies was confined to the exercise of seven possible options: oral reprimand; written reprimand; punishment duty (work without pay); transfer; suspension; termination; and prosecution. Officers could be disciplined with little or no consideration for their constitutional rights and, in many instances, were disciplined in an arbitrary and capricious manner. Because of some outrageously unfair disciplinary practices, the courts and the National Labor Relations Board outlawed numerous unfair labor practices and provided officers relief in the courts (i.e., the N.L.R.B. decision in the Garcia case, which outlawed punishment duty and the United States Supreme Court decision in Patsy v. Florida Board of

Regents, which guaranteed persons in the process of being disciplined the right to initiate litigation in the federal courts for violation of their civil rights "without exhausting administrative remedies provided under the state law"). Many states also passed "Police Officer Bill of Rights" statutes. (p. 233)

Over time, both in Canada and the United States, more positive and constructive approaches have come into place. There is now a greater reliance on training, guidance, and counselling to remedy any problems with officer performance. However, because it remains true that officers do commit violations for personal and vindictive reasons, there continues to be a need for processes designed to address these actions through some form of due process and punishment.

In attempting to explain the continuing need for police discipline, the Ontario Civilian Commission on Police Services (1992) offers the following statement:

> Police officers are only human. As in every other line of work, some of them on occasion will get into trouble. The test of the integrity of a police force is not that all its officers be perfect, but that when there are allegations of misconduct, they are dealt with quickly, fairly and openly. (p. 4)

The Ontario Civilian Commission on Police Services (1992), in its review of the internal discipline processes within the Metropolitan Toronto Police Service, made some observations that speak to the systemic problem of having internal mechanisms that do not come under the scrutiny of civilian oversight bodies. It becomes highly problematic when a public service does not share publicly the details of its disciplinary actions and deliberations. Accordingly, the evidence that the commission heard relevant to the Metropolitan Toronto Police could be extended to every police service in Ontario:

> The evidence put before this Inquiry has revealed that:
> - There has been a tendency by the force to treat cases involving errant officers as an in-house problem, rather than a matter of public concern.
> - In an effort to rid the force of an officer who was considered unsuitable, expediency has taken precedence over principle.
> - Accountability for police discipline and civilian review has been compromised.
> - Inadequate consideration has been given to victims of police wrongdoing. (p. 6)

And further:

> The Supreme Court of Canada has distinguished between matters of a public nature, intended to promote public order and welfare within a public sphere of activity, and disciplinary matters which are regulatory, protective or corrective and which are primarily intended to maintain discipline, professional integrity and professional standards or to regulate conduct within a limited private sphere of activity. (Wigglesworth v. Her Majesty the Queen; Burnham v. Ackroyd et al.; Re Imrie and Institute of Chartered Accountants of Ontario). (p. 11)

SOME CASES OF INTEREST

There are a number of significant decisions that have been rendered over the last few years that have a bearing on the topic of police discipline in Canada. The following cases have been selected in order to provide a sample of the kinds of issues and concerns that have arisen when individual officers have breached various elements of the code of conduct. They are representative of the broad range of concerns that challenge police executives and which are of vital importance to civilian governors, as well as the public at large.

The Ontario Civilian Commission on Police Services (OCCPS) has been extensively discussed in previous chapters. Here we will look at some of the disciplinary decisions rendered by the OCCPS to better understand how police discipline works in the province of Ontario. The OCCPS is a model for other jurisdictions; therefore, it is highly instructive to consider the types of disciplinary decisions reported by this quasi-judicial body. What follows is a list of relevant cases and a summary of each:

- Case of Gordon Junger;
- Case of Brian Whitehead;
- Case of Constable Turgeon;
- Case of Constables E. Hewitt and C. Devine;
- Case of Constable Perry Mason;
- Case of Detective Sergeant Jack More; and
- Case of Sergeant Gary Lewin.

CASE OF GORDON JUNGER

In 1989, Gordon Junger began a relationship with Ms. Roma Langford, who was a prostitute. Junger has been a member of the Metropolitan Toronto Police since 1980 and was attached to No. 52 Division. He began living with Langford and the fact of this co-habitation came to the attention of the Internal Affairs unit in July 1989.

In the fall of that year, Junger and Langford started an escort agency, "Pleasure Can Be Yours Escort Service," and advertised for clients and employees. In December, Langford informed the Internal Affairs unit of Junger's involvement with the service and made other allegations of discreditable conduct and dereliction of duty. She further indicated that Junger was using narcotics and had screened prospective employees for the escort service using the Canadian Police Information Centre (CPIC). Following a sting operation where Junger accepted money from a female police officer posing as a client looking for sexual services, he was arrested on a criminal charge of living off the avails of prostitution.

No criminal or disciplinary charges for the unauthorized use of the CPIC were laid and no written brief on the investigation was sent to the Trials Preparation Unit for the purpose of laying *Police Act* charges.

In January 1990, investigators with the Internal Affairs unit met with Junger's lawyer. They discussed the terms of an agreement that would provide for his resignation from the force, the withdrawal of outstanding possession charges, and the destruction of all physical evidence relating to the investigation. Furthermore, if a third party asked for a reference for Junger, the Toronto Police would use a form letter simply referring to when he commenced employment, the capacity in which he served, the date he ceased employment, and his position at the time of leaving the employ of the force. This agreement was to be kept confidential.

The Internal Affairs unit found many aspects of this matter to be unsatisfactory and presented a series of recommendations to address some of the deficiencies and failures in this regard.

CASE OF BRIAN WHITEHEAD

On November 7, 1989, Sergeant Brian Whitehead, who had been a member of the Metropolitan Toronto Police since 1967, picked up a prostitute, Jane Doe. This woman subsequently arranged a meeting with the Internal Affairs unit and alleged that an officer, whose name she did not know, had extorted sexual services from her upon a threat of arrest. Such actions on the part of an officer could involve criminal offences of sexual assault and extortion, as well as corrupt practices and deceit, all of which are covered in the Code of Offences under the *Police Act* (the precursor to the *Police Services Act*).

Jane Doe indicated that she wanted the officer in question punished in some manner and requested that her identity be kept confidential. An immediate investigation was launched to learn the identity of the officer in question. Recording equipment was installed on Jane Doe's telephone and Sergeant Whitehead was arrested at Jane Doe's apartment on November 23, 1989, on charges of sexual assault and extortion.

Although under arrest, Whitehead was not formally interrogated or fingerprinted in connection with the offences for which he was arrested. No criminal information was sworn and no arrest report or Crown brief was prepared. Whitehead was allowed to go home after three hours without a formal release from arrest.

In February 1990, charges of corrupt practice (i.e., using one's position as a member of the police service for private advantage) and deceit (making a false, misleading, or inaccurate statement to another officer) were laid against Whitehead. Jane Doe's identity was revealed on the charge sheets and she was not notified of the proceedings or the date of the appearances. The Hearing Officer sentenced Whitehead to a reduction in rank from sergeant to first class constable. In May 1990 the chief of police reviewed and confirmed the conviction and the sentence.

In the remaining five cases, the findings of the Ontario Civilian Commission on Police Services were appealed.

CASE OF CONSTABLE TURGEON

Appellant: Constable Turgeon
Respondent: Ontario Provincial Police
Hearing date: July 1999

Constable Turgeon appeals a finding of unlawful or unnecessary exercise of authority contrary to section 1(g)(ii) of the Code of Conduct contained in Regulation 927 of the Revised Regulations of Ontario 1990. He also appeals the penalty of forfeiture of ten days' paid time.

BACKGROUND

Officers stopped a blue minivan and learned that the driver was a young offender unlawfully at large. It also became apparent that the van was stolen and that the young offender, ET, did not have a driver's licence. Constable Turgeon pushed ET, causing his head and body to hit the side of the vehicle. ET was handcuffed and placed in the police cruiser. Before this, however, Constable Turgeon noticed that ET was wearing a bracelet and asked him if this item was stolen. ET denied that it was stolen and Constable Turgeon said that if he didn't tell him the truth he would take him into the bush and make him talk.

During the questioning that followed, Constable Turgeon struck ET in the face. The accompanying officer spoke to his sergeant about Constable Turgeon's behaviour and was informed that this behaviour was serious and warranted an investigation.

DECISION

The Hearing Officer in this case found that Constable Turgeon used overly severe and unnecessary violence against ET. Also, a threat had been uttered when the constable told ET that if he did not confess to the theft of the bracelet he would be made to talk. The officer's actions were deemed to be discreditable and a penalty was imposed. An appeal was made on the grounds that the penalty was excessive. The OCCPS offered the following comments on the issue:

> On the issue of penalty, it is important to take into account prior disciplinary cases dealing with similar types of misconduct to ensure consistency. There are other factors, which can be relevant either mitigating or aggravating the penalty, depending on the particular conduct in question.

These include provocation, the need for deterrence and concerns arising from management's approach to the misconduct in question.

It was concluded that Constable Turgeon showed no remorse and a lack of regard for his supervisors. The decision of the Hearing Officer was upheld and the appeal dismissed.

CASE OF CONSTABLES E. HEWITT AND C. DEVINE

Appellants: Constables E. Hewitt and C. Devine
Respondent: Toronto Police Service
Hearing date: August 1999

Constables E. Hewitt and C. Devine appeal their convictions on charges of neglect of duty contrary to section I(c)(i) of the Code of Conduct contained in Regulation 927. They further appeal the penalty imposed of forfeiture of three days' or 24 hours' paid time.

BACKGROUND

Officers received a radio call dispatching them to attend at a location where there were persons in a van behaving suspiciously. The vehicle was reported stolen. The officers scouted the area but did not locate the van. They found a pool cue and a baseball bat, which they placed in the trunk of their cruiser. The officers returned to other duties without reporting their findings to the dispatcher. At the end of their shift, the officers filed no seized property report and left the pool cue and the baseball bat in the trunk of the cruiser.

DECISION

Both officers were charged with neglect of duty and insubordination contrary to section 1(b)(ii) of the Code for carrying out an order without lawful excuse. This related to failing to complete a property receipt and a form for the recovered pool cue and baseball bat, contrary to Directive 09-01 of the Policy and Procedure Manual.

The officers concluded after being on the scene that the incident was neither serious nor crime-related. The opinion of the OCCPS was that the officers had no compelling reason to call into their dispatcher something that the officers both considered trivial. There was a report that other officers were investigating a similar attack in that area, but the officers in this case were unaware of that investigation.

As a result, the appeal was allowed and the penalties imposed by the Hearing Officer were quashed.

CASE OF CONSTABLE PERRY MASON

Appellant: Constable Perry Mason
Respondent: Hamilton-Wentworth Regional Police Service
Hearing date: November 1999

Constable Mason appeals the penalty of reduction in rank for six months to second class constable imposed for the offence of discreditable conduct contrary to section 1(a)(ix) of Regulation 927 Revised Regulations of Ontario 1990 as amended (the Code).

Background

Constable Mason was found guilty of uttering a death threat contrary to the *Criminal Code of Canada*. This threat had been directed against a staff sergeant with the Hamilton-Wentworth Regional Police Service while both men were at a hockey arena and off duty.

The officer was separated from his wife, who had custody of their child. Mason had earlier agreed not to enter the arena dressing room when his wife brought the child to the arena. He did and the coach asked him to leave after Mason became abusive and irate. He began swearing and creating a scene, and the police were called. The staff sergeant was in the arena at the time with his own child and attempted to deal with Mason. Mason cursed the staff sergeant and threatened his life. The staff sergeant left the arena.

Decision

Mason's actions were seen as being contrary to section 264.1(1) of the *Criminal Code*, which relates to the uttering of threats. The punishment for this offence ranges from a term not exceeding eighteen months (on summary conviction) to a term of imprisonment not exceeding five years (on conviction of an indictable offence).

There was a previous informal discipline report on Mason for an earlier incident of discreditable conduct. The Hearing Officer stated in his decision that the stress Mason was under due to the breakdown of his marriage was regrettable, but could not be used as an excuse for inappropriate behaviour and that police officers are expected to deal with the stress of their personal and professional lives.

In assessing a penalty, the Hearing Officer took into account the value of:

- General deterrence;
- Specific deterrence;
- Rehabilitation; and
- Progressive discipline.

code. There is typically a great deal of anxiety that attends these events, both within the ranks and among the police executive. It is not unusual for these matters to have a relatively significant public profile, and this includes sometimes intense media attention as the case moves through the various stages of hearings and possible appeals. Therefore, it is important to deal with the systemic impact of disciplinary proceedings and be aware of their impact on the individuals and the organization. Again, Sheehan and Cordner (1995) are helpful in considering the overall philosophy of police discipline:

> In considering disciplinary measures, the police manager must now carefully weigh disciplinary objectives and employee relations as well as legal issues and constraints before taking disciplinary action. In all but the most blatantly serious situations, every effort should be made to place emphasis on redemption, rehabilitation and reform, not punishment. (p. 233)

The U.S. National Advisory Commission on Criminal Justice Standards and Goals (1973) recommended that there be formalized approaches to investigating citizen complaints against the police. In order to minimize any negative impacts, procedures for police discipline should include considerations of:

- *Certainty*—the inevitability of punishment may serve as a strong deterrent to police misconduct;
- *Swiftness*—delays in the investigation of alleged misconduct tend to weaken any system of discipline and place an undue burden of anxiety on the subject officers and other police colleagues. It also speaks to lack of decisiveness on the part of the supervisor;
- *Fairness and impartiality*—there should be an equitable application of any system of police discipline, and supervisors must be able to set personal feelings aside for this purpose; and
- *Consistency*—conduct of a certain variety should always be met with punishment of a similar variety in all cases; however, aggravating and/or mitigating circumstances should be taken into account within the context of the individual officer's past performance record. Overly severe or excessively lenient discipline might create an environment that is not productive.

Within the positive framework, Glensor, Peak, and Haines (1999) have noted the following important administrative, supervisory, and leadership elements when developing effective disciplinary processes:

- Adequate training and retraining;
- Publicized rules of ethics and conduct;
- Consistent leadership and supervision;
- Coaching and counselling;

- Regular performance evaluations; and
- Prompt corrective action against inappropriate attitudes and conduct.

Discipline is a tool for supervisors to ensure that the department runs smoothly and that approved policies and procedures are observed. Ideally, every police service seeks to construct an organization where employees are guided by realistic policies, practices, and procedures in a way that ensures they exhibit voluntary compliance (Glensor, Peak, and Haines, 1999, p. 215) without the need for punitive forms of discipline.

Positive discipline (also known as progressive discipline or positive counselling) attempts to change employee behaviour without invoking punishment. Negative discipline involves punishment and is generally invoked when positive disciplinary measures have been applied unsuccessfully.

Historically, it was seen as essential for the purposes of public confidence in the police that there be explicit and detailed codes of conduct to guide police behaviour and to provide for any necessary disciplinary action. Philips (1983) makes this point:

> Within the English constitutional context of government it is not surprising that, when the trained semi-professional police with new powers were first introduced into London in 1829, the force should at once have been required to operate under a formal code of discipline governing police behaviour; nor that the introduction of the code should simultaneously have been associated with arrangements providing for complaints by the public. From the start the police were required to be accountable. (p. 108)

THE RCMP EXTERNAL REVIEW COMMITTEE

In relation to our federal police agency, the Royal Canadian Mounted Police, the RCMP External Review Committee is guided by the *RCMP External Review Committee Rules of Practice and Procedure* (SOR/88-313, 8 June 1988; as amended by SOR/91-544, 17 September 1991; and SOR/97-437, 16 September 1997). This committee forms a component of a two-level redress mechanism available to members of the RCMP who are not satisfied with disciplinary actions, discharges, or demotions, or with other RCMP decisions, acts, or omissions which impact upon their employee rights and for which no other redress process is provided by the *RCMP Act* or its regulations.

The committee independently reviews grievances and appeals referred to it and submits recommendations to the RCMP commissioner, who acts as the second and last level of the review process. The RCMP commissioner is not required to accept the recommendations of the committee, but when she or he chooses not to do so, she or he is required to provide reasons. The commissioner's decision is final, although it is subject to judicial review by the Federal Court.

Under the *RCMP Act*, the RCMP commissioner refers all appeals of formal discipline and all discharge and demotion appeals to the committee unless the member of the RCMP requests that the matter not be referred. In addition, pursuant to section 33 of the *RCMP Act*, the RCMP commissioner refers certain types of grievances to the committee in accordance with regulations made by the Governor in Council. Section 36 of the RCMP regulations specifies the grievances that the RCMP commissioner is obliged to refer to the committee, namely:

- The Force's interpretation and application of government policies that apply to government departments and that have been made to apply to members;
- The stoppage of pay and allowances of members made pursuant to subsection 22(3) of the *RCMP Act*;
- The Force's interpretation and application of the Isolated Posts Directive;
- The Force's interpretation and application of the RCMP Relocation Directive; and
- Administrative discharge on the grounds of physical or mental disability, abandonment of post, or irregular appointment.

The RCMP External Review Committee is a component of the federal Ministry of the Solicitor General and reports annually to Parliament. Its stakeholders are the members of the RCMP. The committee adheres to the following objective and strategic priorities:

Objective:

The committee's main objective is to provide Canadians with assurances of the protection of RCMP members' rights, by way of civilian oversight of the RCMP in certain matters pertaining to labour relations within the RCMP.

Strategic Priorities:

The Committee is committed to providing the Commissioner with impartial, useful, and timely advice on specific matters referred to it, by:

- Conducting its reviews in a manner that respects and balances the interests of the RCMP, its members and members of the Canadian public;
- Developing and maintaining the trust and confidence of RCMP management and members that each case will receive an impartial review; and
- Constantly reviewing its mandate with a view to further improving the openness, accountability and efficiency of the grievance/appeal process.

ONTARIO

In Ontario, there are a number of elements that police officers, and police administrators, need to understand with respect to police discipline. The *Police Services Act* contains two discipline provisions: substantiated complaints and hearings.

SUBSTANTIATED COMPLAINTS

When a chief of police receives an investigation report that substantiates a complaint, he or she has two options for proceeding. The chief may take remedial action with the consent of both the member of the police force and the investigator without formally charging the member with a disciplinary offence. Or, the chief must charge the member with a minor or major disciplinary offence and order a hearing into the matter. However, if the member is convicted of an offence that might render that member unsuitable for service, the chief may take other actions.

HEARINGS

The complainant may attend a hearing and may be represented by legal counsel at the complainant's expense. A Hearing Officer, appointed by the Lieutenant Governor in Council, conducts a hearing. The Hearing Officer must be either a lawyer in good standing with any law society in Canada for five years preceding the appointment, or have been a member of the judiciary.

The Hearing Officer has a broad range of sanction powers for a major disciplinary offence by a member or chief, including:

- Dismissal from the force;
- Demotion;
- Suspension up to 60 days without pay;
- A fine not exceeding $1000;
- A probationary period or close supervision;
- Counselling, treatment, or training;
- A reprimand;
- Any other order the Hearing Officer deems fit and any combination of the above-noted sanctions; or
- Dismissal of the matter.

The Hearing Officer has a narrower range of sanctions for minor disciplinary offences by a member or chief, namely:

- Probation or close supervision;
- A fine not exceeding $200;
- Counselling, treatment, or training;
- Any other order the Hearing Officer deems fit and any combination of the above-listed sanctions; or
- Dismissal of the matter.

The *Police Services Act* allows for a 30-day period, after the day on which notice was given, for the member, chief, board, or complainant to apply to the commission for leave to appeal the Hearing Officer's decision. This is not an automatic right of appeal.

NEW BRUNSWICK

The following provides a fairly lengthy reproduction of the provisions of the police discipline regulations for the province of New Brunswick. However, it is extremely useful for the reader to examine, and understand, the extent to which legislators and regulators have gone to circumscribe police behaviour. The material extracted below provides an exhaustive listing of all the circumstances under which an officer will be deemed to have acted improperly; and, by extension, it is a guide to proper action on the part of a police officer. A considerable amount of thought has gone into the formulation of Section 38 of the Discipline Regulation 86-49, Part 2, which states:

Whereas it is incumbent upon every police officer within the Province to:

(a) respect the rights of all persons,
(b) maintain the integrity of the law, law enforcement and the administration of justice,
(c) perform his duties promptly, impartially and diligently in accordance with the law and without abusing his authority,
(d) avoid any actual, apparent or potential conflict of interest,
(e) ensure that any unlawful conduct of any member is not concealed or permitted to continue,
(e.1) ensure that any improper conduct of any member when performing the duties of a police officer is not concealed or permitted to continue,
(f) be incorruptible, never accepting or seeking special privilege in the performance of his duties or otherwise placing himself under any obligation that may prejudice the proper performance of his duties, and
(g) conduct himself at all times in a manner that will not bring discredit on his role as a police officer

Section 39 of Discipline Regulation 86-49 states:

No police officer shall

(a) use abusive language or oppressive conduct toward another police officer;
(b) willfully or negligently make any false complaint or statement against a police officer;
(c) withhold or suppress a complaint or report alleging wrongdoing by himself or another police officer;
(d) contravene section 6, 12, 21, 22 or 36 of the *Act* or any order or regulation made under the *Act*;
(e) be insubordinate to his supervisors;
(f) without lawful excuse, refuse, neglect, omit or fail to carry out any lawful order;
(g) neglect or omit to promptly and diligently perform his duties as a police officer;

(h) fail to discharge his responsibilities in accordance with the instructions received;

(i) be absent from duty without reasonable excuse;

(j) by carelessness or neglect permit a prisoner to escape;

(k) willfully or negligently make a false, misleading or inaccurate statement, oral or written, with intent to mislead
  (i) a police officer,
  (ii) any person in authority;

(l) willfully make any false or misleading entry in any document, record or report required to be completed in the course of his duties;

(m) willfully and without lawful authority, destroy, mutilate, alter, erase, remove, conceal or make any additions to any official police document or record;

(n) being a chief of police, fail to comply with subsection 12(2.1) of the *Act*;

(o) without proper authority or just cause, disclose directly or indirectly to any person, information which he has acquired while a police officer;

(p) directly or indirectly, with intent that any person may escape the due process of law, give to any person, notice that a warrant or summons has been or is about to be issued;

(q) fail to properly account for, or make a prompt and true return of any money or other property received by him in the course of his duty;

(r) in his capacity as a police officer and without the consent of his chief of police directly or indirectly solicit or receive an gratuity, gift, subscription or testimonial;

(s) place himself under a pecuniary or other obligation to any person in such a manner as might affect the proper performance of his duties as a police officer;

(t) without lawful authority, make any arrest or detain any person;

(u) be discourteous or disrespectful toward any member of the public;

(v) use any unnecessary force upon or apply cruel treatment to any prisoner or any other person with whom he may come into contact in the performance of his duties;

(w) upon discharging a firearm while on duty, other than at a bona fide firearm training exercise authorized by his chief of police, fail to file a complete police report during his current tour of duty;

(x) fail to exercise discretion and restraint in the use and care of firearms;

(y) willfully or negligently cause any waste, loss or damage to police force property coming into his possession by virtue of his office as a police officer;

(z) without lawful authorization of his chief of police loan, give, sell or otherwise deliver to any person, other than a police officer, any piece of police uniform or equipment;

(aa) have been found guilty by a court of competent jurisdiction of an offence under the Criminal Code, chapter C-34 of the *Revised Statutes of Canada*, 1970; the *Food and Drugs Act*, chapter F-27 of the *Revised Statutes of Canada*, 1970; or the *Narcotic Control Act*, chapter N-1 of the *Revised Statutes of Canada*, 1970;

(bb) fail to search a person taken into custody for the purpose of lawfully removing
  (i) any item that may be used as evidence, or
  (ii) any instrument or other thing that could be used to cause harm to any person or facilitate an escape;

(cc) fail to offer evidence that he is capable of disclosing for or against any person charged with an offence under a statute of Canada or a Provincial statute;

(dd) use or attempt to use his position as a police officer for private advantage;

(ee) without the permission of his chief of police, carry, while on duty, any firearm or other equipment, other than equipment issued to him by the police force of which he is a member; or

(ff) report for duty or continue on duty while unfit to perform his duties as a result of having consumed or ingested intoxicating liquor or drugs.

Every police officer who violates a provision of subsection (1) commits a major violation of the code.

Section 40 of Discipline Regulation 86-49, states:

(1) No police officer shall

(c) sign or circulate a petition or statement in respect of a matter concerning a police force, except through
   (i) the official channels of correspondence within the police force,
   (ii) established grievance procedure pursuant to a collective agreement then in force, or
   (iii) in the bona fide performance of his duties as a representative of a union, association or federation;

(d) [REPEALED]

(e) without the consent of his chief of police, support in his capacity as a police officer any application by another party for a licence of any kind;

(f) while on duty, undertake or make any attempt to effect the service or execution of documents involved in a civil process without the authorization of his chief of police;

(g) [REPEALED]

(h) have possession of a firearm or other restricted or prohibited weapon issued by the police force of which he is a member except for the purposes of his duties or employment as a police officer;

(i) fail to file a complete report to his chief of police through proper channels, or in the case of the chief of police, to the board or council or the Minister, as the case may be, of any loss of or damage to property that is in his possession by virtue of his office as a police officer or as a chief of police;

(j) while on duty, be untidy in his person, uniform, clothing or equipment;

(k) appear in public dressed partly in police uniform and partly in civilian attire;

(l) wear his uniform while off duty or on leave without the authorization of the chief of police or his delegate;

(m) [REPEALED]

(n) have been found guilty by a court of competent jurisdiction of an offence involving moral turpitude under
   (i) a statute of Canada, except the statutes referred to in paragraph 39(1)(aa), or
   (ii) a statute of a Province or Territory within Canada. . . .

(o) for remuneration, be involved directly or indirectly in the sale or distribution of intoxicating liquor, if the person from whom the police officer receives such remuneration has, within the last twelve months,
   (i) had a licence or permit cancelled or suspended under the *Liquor Control Act*,
   (ii) been found guilty of an offence under the *Liquor Control Act*, the *Food and Drugs Act*, chapter F-27 of the *Revised Statutes of Canada*, 1970; or the *Narcotics Control Act*, chapter N-1 of the *Revised Statutes of Canada*, 1970.

Every police officer who violates a provision of subsection (1) commits a minor violation of the code.

MANITOBA

Penalties for an officer found guilty of any of the identified disciplinary defaults established by the Law Enforcement Review Agency (LERA) are outlined below in diminishing order of seriousness:

- Dismissal;
- Permission to resign and, in default of resignation within seven days, summary dismissal;
- Reduction in rank;
- Suspension without pay up to a maximum of 30 days;
- Forfeiture of pay up to a maximum of 10 days' pay;
- Forfeiture of leave or days off not to exceed 10 days;
- Written reprimand;
- Verbal reprimand; or
- Admonition.

POLICE ETHICS

The overall topic of ethics has been of growing interest in the context of many human endeavours. Groups representing doctors, lawyers, teachers, and other professionals have been turning their attention to the need for more rigorous and more clearly defined codes of ethical behaviour. For example, in Ontario, the Ontario College of Teachers was formed in 1996 to provide a focal point for sustaining ethical standards within the teaching profession and to administer the provisions of the disciplinary regulations under the *Ontario College of Teachers Act*. In policing, the topics of ethics and character have become significant and are frequently featured as the focus of police conferences, workshops, and learning seminars. However, ethics is a subject that has been studied since the most ancient of days, for example, by Socrates, Plato, and Aristotle. So what accounts for this newfound interest?

With the erosion of public trust that has plagued many institutions over the last several decades, there has been a growing interest in the ethical dimension. Also, as technology has made it easier for us to transform the world around us, we have become uncertain about the standards of right and wrong that might apply. This is seen particularly in the world of medical research where issues of genetic research, cloning, experiments with fetal stem-cell tissues, and transplants have introduced complex questions that must be addressed. In the realm of politics, where politicians have committed acts that betray the public trust, or have appeared to breach the unspoken code of decency with respect to their private affairs, we have been moved to question the ethical principles we wish to live by as a collective. All of these concerns have impacted on police leaders,

Police officers are held to a high ethical standard.

who have responsibility for ensuring that their organizations function in a manner that is consistent with the ethical standards of society at large. The police themselves, their civilian governors, the legislators (both federal and provincial), and the public all have an important interest in the standards of ethical action that police organizations foster and observe. Accordingly, ethics is a topic of significant importance to anyone seeking a career in policing in Canada.

In a sense, notions of ethics and character should rightly precede any consideration of police discipline. This is true for the simple reason that if all police officers and all police organizations observed clear standards of ethics and integrity, there would be little need for a disciplinary regime. With people of character observing internalized rules of good conduct and right action, misconduct would be essentially unknown. Edwin Delattre (1998), who has written widely, and wisely, on the topic of police ethics, makes the following observation:

> Acquiring integrity of character, becoming the kind of person who behaves rightly when not externally forced to do so is what makes a person thoroughly and profoundly worthy of trust in public and private life. For this reason, integrity properly understood is irreplaceable as the foundation of good friendships, good marriages, good parenthood, good sportsmanship, good citizenship, and good public service. (p. 3)

Strong leadership in the area of police ethics has been shown in recent years by the Canadian Association of Chiefs of Police (CACP). Because this organization represents the issues and interests of all police organizations across the country, it is useful to consider the association's efforts at coming to terms with the current challenge pertaining to ethical standards for police. Recently, the CACP has been engaged in dialogue and discussion to frame its own understanding of this dimension of policing. The association has come to the view that the development of a code of ethics will set forth a range of values that will be important for police leaders. The CACP has committed itself to advocating the highest professional and ethical standards for policing across Canada. In fact, ethical reasoning skills have been identified as a core competency requirement for police leaders. Integrity, too, has been labelled as an important characteristic by several police agencies. The Human Resources Committee of the CACP has been guiding an initiative to examine and update the CACP's Code of Ethics for national application.

The CACP's ethical framework, which has been approved in principle, identifies four key client groups in the working life of a police leader: public; police staff and organization; professional partners; and personal. The ethical foundation for these responsibilities and relationships is drawn from the following fundamental values:

- Democratic principles;
- Human dignity;
- The rule of law; and
- A moral core.

A three-dimensional pyramid has been constructed to represent this ethical framework rooted in the ethical foundation noted above. The four faces of this pyramid are represented in Figures 3.1, 3.2, 3.3, and 3.4.

As part of his work with the British Columbia Office of Police Complaints, Dr. Eike-Henner W. Kluge (1999a) articulated the following ethical principles, which certainly have application to police work:

- *Autonomy and respect for person*: everyone has the right to self-determination subject only to the equal and competing rights of others;
- *Equality and justice*: every person is the equal of every other person qua person, and has the right to be treated the same;
- *Integrity/best action*: everyone is obliged to fulfill his or her duties in the best way possible; and
- *Beneficence and non-malfeasance*: there lies a general duty to advance the good and prevent harm.

Furthermore, Kluge (1999c) observes that:

In an ethical sense, police agencies are the administrative embodiments of society's desire to maintain law and order. Since these agencies are expected to function in a quasi-independent fashion, they stand in a fiduciary relationship toward society. They have a duty to uphold the standards and values that are enshrined in (or are provided for by) legislation, regulations, procedures and to do so in a manner that is consonant with the ethical principles that govern all conduct within a social context. . . . In particular, the values that are here implicated include:

FIGURE 3.1

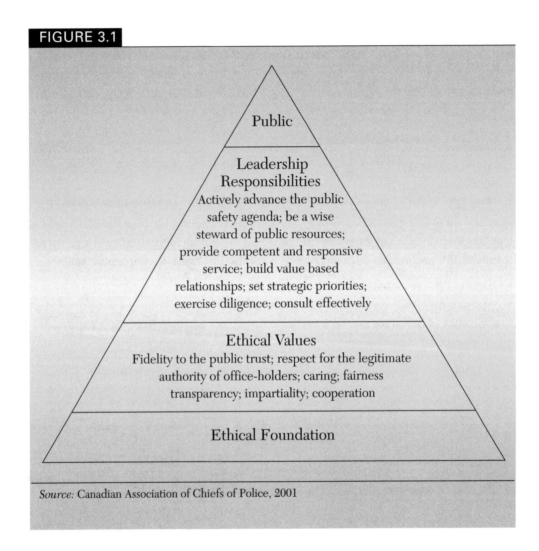

Source: Canadian Association of Chiefs of Police, 2001

- truthfulness;
- openness and transparency of operation;
- trustworthiness;
- accountability;
- preservation of rights; and
- protection of public welfare. (p. 5)

When considering ethical questions, it is important to realize that police organizations have an enormous responsibility to bear in the context of the public trust. Police officers are given a significant degree of discretion and control over the lives of their fellow citizens. They operate in ways that are frequently outside the direct and immediate

FIGURE 3.2

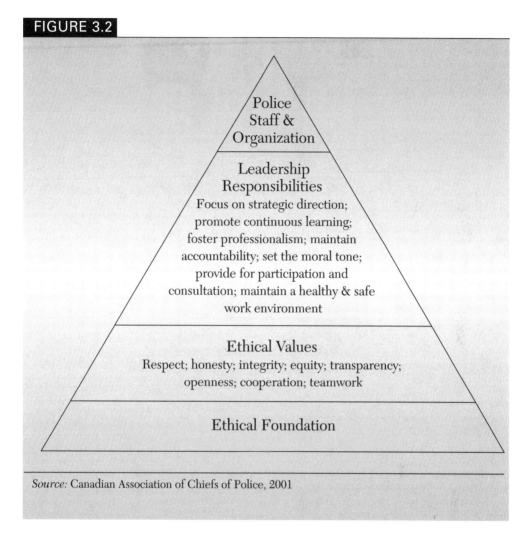

Police Staff & Organization

Leadership Responsibilities
Focus on strategic direction; promote continuous learning; foster professionalism; maintain accountability; set the moral tone; provide for participation and consultation; maintain a healthy & safe work environment

Ethical Values
Respect; honesty; integrity; equity; transparency; openness; cooperation; teamwork

Ethical Foundation

Source: Canadian Association of Chiefs of Police, 2001

supervision of their senior officers and must, therefore, rely on their own personal standards of ethical behaviour and proper conduct. While Canada has not had any instances quite as explosive as the beating of Rodney King (by officers of the Los Angeles Police Department), there is never room for complacency when it comes to possible police corruption, brutality, or misconduct. It is vital that all police officers understand that character, integrity, and ethical action are central to their role as public servants, and as human beings. Because we could never have enough supervisors to ensure that all police behaviour is monitored and observed, we must try to ensure that each officer is imbued with the ethical principles that make right action part of his or her nature and not something merely derived from a rule book or a code of conduct.

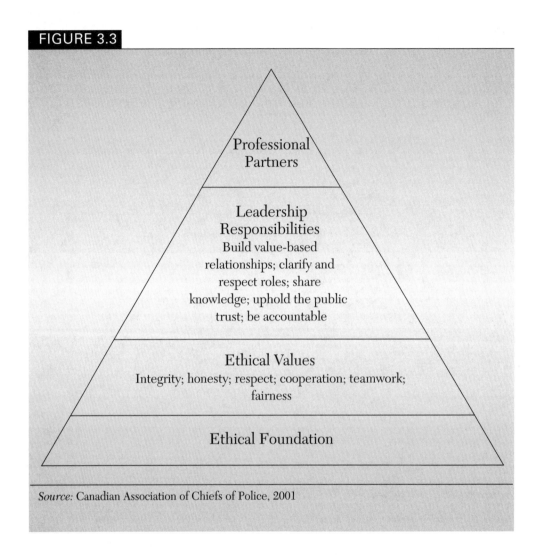

FIGURE 3.3

Source: Canadian Association of Chiefs of Police, 2001

CONCLUSION

This chapter has attempted to provide an overall perspective on the issue of police discipline. It has looked at how police organizations, and the appropriate civilian oversight bodies, actually deal with police officers who have engaged in conduct that is unethical, unlawful, unwarranted, or unauthorized. We have considered a number of specific cases where officers have been charged with corrupt practices or discreditable conduct and have examined the decisions rendered in these specific instances. Also, we have looked briefly at the important topic of police ethics. The treatment provided here has been highly provisional; however, it is essential that students of

FIGURE 3.4

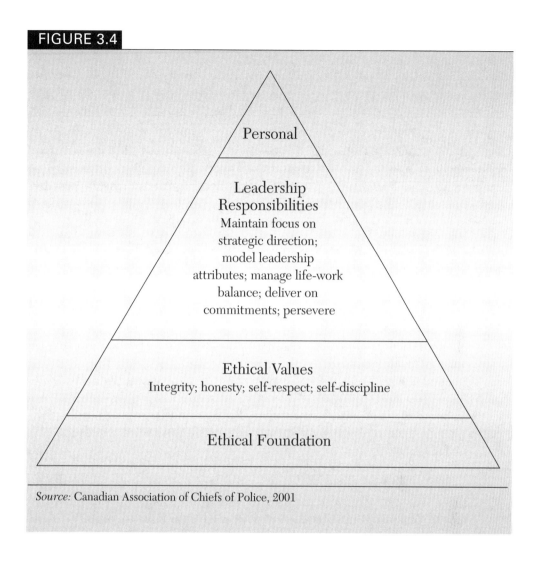

Personal

Leadership
Responsibilities
Maintain focus on
strategic direction;
model leadership
attributes; manage life-work
balance; deliver on
commitments; persevere

Ethical Values
Integrity; honesty; self-respect; self-discipline

Ethical Foundation

Source: Canadian Association of Chiefs of Police, 2001

policing in Canada be fully aware of this topic as a cornerstone of their learning about the why's and wherefore's of professional policing.

Discipline is the response to unethical or unprofessional action on the part of police officers, while ethics is the means by which police organizations can prepare police officers to operate in a manner that will preclude the need for disciplinary action. If all police organizations invested time, energy, and interest in the process of instilling and supporting high ethical standards, there would be far less need to expend human effort in the exercise of disciplinary tribunals, and the cycle of anxiety and uncertainty imposed by the need for remedial actions could be broken.

Policing is a profoundly demanding and difficult job. It has the potential for depriving people of their liberty, and, at an extreme, their lives. Therefore, it is essential that police officers be people of the highest moral quality, either by nurture or by training. Every time an officer is found guilty of some form of corrupt or unethical practice, the organization they represent is tarnished by association. Every time one police officer is found to be operating in a manner that is not consistent with the public good, the reasonable person may be forgiven for speculating that policing is not a profession that conforms itself to high universal values. If one police officer can function in a way that is unworthy of our trust and respect, all officers must be prepared to account for themselves in the court of public opinion.

QUESTIONS FOR CONSIDERATION AND DISCUSSION

1. How is it possible to ensure that internal police discipline procedures are fair?
2. What distinguishes misconduct from criminal behaviour?
3. What are some of the key considerations for any system of police discipline?
4. What is progressive discipline?
5. What are the types of sanctions available for major disciplinary offences under the Ontario *Police Services Act*?
6. What are the types of sanctions available for minor disciplinary offences under the Ontario *Police Services Act*?
7. What forms of punishment exist for discreditable conduct?
8. What might be considered as mitigating or aggravating factors in a police disciplinary case?
9. Why have police organizations been reluctant to make police disciplinary processes open to the public?
10. What is the meaning of "corrupt practices" as it relates to police discipline?
11. What are some key ethical standards that are relevant to police officers in Canada?
12. What can be learned from the case of the two officers from the Saskatoon Police Service who were found guilty of unlawful confinement in connection with the abandonment of an Aboriginal man outside the city limits in January 2000? Discuss the various aspects of this case and the handling of this matter from the following perspectives: the officers, the victim, the police service, the police association, the senior police administration, the community, the media, the larger police community, the province, and the nation.
13. What are the components of the Canadian Association of Chiefs of Police's ethical foundation?
14. What are the moral values that should inform policing in Canada?

RELATED ACTIVITIES

1. Review other decisions of police tribunals, such as the Ontario Civilian Commission on Police Services (OCCPS), and discuss the background and issues they raise for policing.
2. Scan the news media for instances of police disciplinary hearings and their outcomes.
3. Compare disciplinary regimes in different jurisdictions across Canada.
4. Compare police codes of conduct in Canada with those in place in other countries, for example, the United States, Great Britain, and Australia.
5. Look at trials for police corruption and consider some of the Commissions of Inquiry that have been established.
6. Read some of the literature on police ethics, and organize discussions on the critical issues that are found in that literature.
7. Debate some of the key ethical dilemmas that confront police officers and consider the complexities and ambiguities of moral action.
8. Look at some of the other professions that have ethical standards and make comparisons between their standards and the standards established for police organizations in Canada. What are the similarities? What are the differences?
9. Compare ethical approaches to policing adopted in Canada to those adopted in other jurisdictions, for example, the United States, Great Britain, and Australia.

REFERENCES

Barker, T. and D.L. Carter (1994). *Police deviance*. Cincinnati, Ohio: Anderson Publishing Co.

Bayley, D.H. (1983). "Accountability and control of the police: some lessons for Britain." In Bennett, T. (ed.) *The future of policing*. Cambridge: Institute of Criminology. (Cropwood Papers; 15).

Berkow, M. (1996). "Weeding out problem officers." *Police Chief*, Vol. 4, pp. 22–29.

Boyer, Peter J. (2001). "Bad cops." *New Yorker*, May 21, 2001, pp. 60–77.

Black, J.M. (1986). *The real meaning of discipline*. Gaithersburg, Md.: International Association of Chiefs of Police.

Chevigny, P. (1969). *Police power: police abuses in New York City*. New York: Vintage Books.

Cohen, Howard S. and Michael Feldberg (1991). *Power and restraint: the moral dimension of police work*. New York: Praeger.

Commission on Accreditation for Law Enforcement agencies (1994). *Standards for law enforcement agencies: the standards manual of the law enforcement accreditation program*. Fairfax, Va.: CALEA.

Delattre, Edwin J. (1994). *Character and cops: ethics in policing*. 2nd ed. Washington, D.C.: American Enterprise Institute for Public Policy Research.

Delattre, Edwin J. (1998). *Ethics in policing*. Ottawa: Police Leadership Forum. (Occasional papers collection).

Elliston, Frederick A. (1984). *Teaching police ethics*. Washington, D.C.: Police Foundation.

Elliston, Frederick A. and Michael Feldberg (eds.) (1985). *Moral issues in police work*. Totowa, N.J.: Rowman & Allanheld.

Gaffigan, S.J. and P.P. McDonald (1997). *Police integrity: public service with honor*. Washington, D.C.: U.S. Dept. of Justice.

Garner, G.W. (1984). "The supervisor's role in discipline." *Law and Order* (March), p. 41.

Giuliani, Rudolph W. and William J. Bratton (1995). "Police strategy no. 7: rooting out corruption: building organizational integrity in the New York City Police department." New York: NYPD. Paper prepared for the NYPD.

Glensor, Ronald W., Kenneth J. Peak, and Larry K. Gaines (1999). *Police supervision*. Boston: McGraw-Hill College.

International Association of Chiefs of Police (1996). "Rooting out corruption and building organizational integrity: the New York experience." Workshop delivered at the 102nd annual IACP conference in Miami, Florida.

Kappeler, Victor E., Richard D. Sluder and Geoffrey P. Alpert (1994). *Forces of deviance: understanding the dark side of policing*. Prospect Heights, Ill.: Waveland Press.

Kleinig, John (1996). *The ethics of policing*. Cambridge: Cambridge University Press.

Kluge, Eike-Henner W. (1999a). *Ethics and policing: opinion of Dr. Eike-Henner W. Kluge: OPCC file #0302*. Victoria, B.C.: Office of the Police Complaint Commissioner.

Kluge, Eike-Henner W. (1999b). *The informal resolution of complaints: ethical considerations*. Victoria, B.C.: Office of the Police Complaint Commissioner.

Kluge, Eike-Henner W. (1999c). *Ethical obligations of police departments in the investigation of police conduct: with particular application to Office of the Police Complaint Commissioner file #0151*. Victoria, B.C.: Office of the Police Complaint Commissioner.

MacNamara, D.E.J. (1985). "Discipline in American policing." In Blumberg, A. and N. Niederhoffer (eds.) *The ambivalent force: perspectives on the police*. New York: Holt, Rinehart & Winston.

Murphy, Patrick V. (1985). "Ethical issues in policing." *Criminal Justice Ethics*, Vol. 4.

New York. Commission to Investigate Allegations of Police Corruption and the City's Anti-Corruption Procedures (1972). *Commission report (with summary and principal recommendations issued August 3, 1972)*. New York: George Braziller.

Ontario Civilian Commission on Police Services (1992). *Report of an inquiry into administration of internal investigations by the Metropolitan Toronto Police Force*. Toronto: The Commission.

Pepinski, Harold E. (1984). "Better living through police discretion." *Law and Contemporary Problems*, Vol. 47.

Police Executive Research Forum (1981). *Police handling of officer misconduct: a model policy statement*. Washington, D.C.: Police Executive Research Forum.

Reiter, B.J. (1979). *Discipline as a means of assuring continuing competence in the professions and tables of discipline activities by profession*. Toronto: The Professional Organizations Committee, Ministry of the Solicitor General.

Royal Canadian Mounted Police External Review Committee (1988). *Suspensions: a balanced view*. Ottawa: Royal Canadian Mounted Police External Review Committee. (Discussion paper; no. 1).

Royal Canadian Mounted Police External Review Committee (1991). *Disciplinary dismissal: a police perspective*. Ottawa: Royal Canadian Mounted Police External Review Committee. (Discussion paper; no. 6).

Royal Canadian Mounted Police External Review Committee (1992). *Conflict of interest*. Ottawa: Royal Canadian Mounted Police External Review Committee.

Sheehan, Robert and Gary W. Cordner (1995). *Police administration*. 3rd edition. Cincinnati, Ohio: Anderson Publishing Co.

Sherman, Lawrence W. (1974). *Police corruption: a sociological perspective*. Garden City, N.J.: Anchor Books.

Sparrow, M.K., M.H. Moore, and D.M. Kennedy (1990). *Beyond 911: a new era for policing*. New York: Basic Books.

Stephens, D.W. (1994). "Discipline philosophy." *FBI Law Enforcement Bulletin*, Vol. 3, pp. 20–22.

Williams, R.N. (1975). *Legal aspects of discipline by police administrators*. Evanston, Ill.: Northwestern University Press. (Traffic Institute publication; no. 2705).

WEBLINKS

 www.erc-cee.gc.ca The RCMP External Review Committee's website contains links to the legislation governing reviews, committee reports, *Communiqué* (the review committee's publication), and discussion papers.

 www.qp.gov.bc.ca/police/r205_98.htm Essential knowledge for police officers, the *Code of Professional Conduct Regulation* (part of the *Police Act*) can be found on this site.

 www.gov.calgary.ab.ca/cpc/pdf/cpcodr.pdf The Review of Police Officer Codes of conduct website provides a review of the conduct of Calgary police officers in their own and other jurisdictions, both on-duty and off, as well as possible sanctions when codes are broken.

 www.polfed.org/magazine/01_2001/01_2001_shootings.htm This site features an article on racism in police shootings by Richard B. Parent (*Police Magazine*, January 2001).

www.freedomtocare.org/page25.htm This website provides users with detailed but generic guidelines for writing codes of ethics and codes of conduct, explaining the substantive, formal, and external considerations that are involved.

CHAPTER FOUR

POLICE LABOUR
RELATIONS IN CANADA

LEARNING OBJECTIVES

1. Describe the key features of union/management relations in Canadian policing.
2. Understand the historical growth of police unions and associations in Canada.
3. Identify some of the key roles police associations in Canada serve with respect to their members.
4. List major areas of justice policy that are pertinent to police associations in Canada.

INTRODUCTION

This chapter will look at the question of police unions, also known as police associations. These are the formally recognized bodies that represent the collective bargaining interests of police officers across Canada. These representative bodies have been in existence for almost as long as there have been police departments in Canada. Furthermore, they have played an important role in the growth and development of policing in this country. It will be useful to examine the history of labour relations in the realm of policing in brief detail, and it is essential that students have a good understanding of the role and function of police unions in a contemporary Canadian setting.

From the earliest days, police unions have found themselves in some degree of conflict with the senior executives of the police hierarchy. For example, the front-line members of the Toronto Police were unionized in 1909 and went on strike in 1918 when several officers refused to give up union membership. It is interesting, however, to compare the growth of police unionism with the evolution of the reform efforts symbolized by the formation in 1905 of the Chief Constables' Association of Canada, which later became the Canadian Association of Chiefs of Police (Marquis, 1993). The 20th century was clearly a time of development and change within Canadian policing, with many groups operating in different ways to seek reform.

The issue of police militancy over the years in Canada has been significant. Strikes occurred in Winnipeg when the police refused to work during the 1919 Winnipeg General Strike. We will see, below, that many police associations have used their collective powers to secure concessions and considerations from police management. We will also observe that many police associations have operated beyond simple matters of employee salaries and benefits and have contributed to the overall improvement of policing and public safety in Canada.

Generally, it can be said that Canadian police services follow an industrial style of labour relations (Forcese, 1992, p. 239). Typically, municipal police associations are linked to some form of provincial body. A good example of this relationship can be found in the case of the Police Association of Ontario (PAO). This organization indirectly represents over 15 000 police officers in the province and will be discussed in more detail below. The national association that represents police associations across Canada is also important. The Canadian Police Association will be examined in more detail later in this chapter.

The notable exception to the rule of police unionism in Canada is the Royal Canadian Mounted Police. The RCMP have not unionized, in spite of several concentrated efforts over the life of this uniquely Canadian institution (Forcese, 1992). The working conditions of RCMP officers and civilian members are overseen by divisional representatives and the RCMP Pay Council (RCMP Pay Council, 1999).

LABOUR/MANAGEMENT RELATIONS

In many ways, police associations have operated over time to erode or alter the previous military model of management that was characteristic of police forces earlier in Canadian history. As representative bodies they have certainly been successful in changing departmental policies and procedures in ways that would not have been imaginable in the early 20th century. Police unions have also functioned to politicize the police in ways that have built important platforms for police associations to speak out on issues of concern to their membership. Such topics include capital punishment, the identification of repeat serious offenders, sentencing laws, the *Young Offenders Act*, and a host of other public safety and criminal justice issues. We will discuss this area in more detail when examining the role of the Canadian Police Association as a national body representing the broad interests of police associations in every jurisdiction of the country.

Police associations have had a lasting and profound impact on the role of the police executive in Canadian policing (Biro et al., 2000). From a survey of recent events in Canada where police associations have targeted their chiefs of police for substantial attack, it is clear that union executives have dispensed with any notion of subservience to the traditional police hierarchy. This has had both beneficial and detrimental impacts on the state of policing in Canada. On the one hand, police associations appear to be attempting to redefine their role in the context of increased professionalism, with a view to taking on greater responsibility for the broader issues in policing. On the other hand, however, there have been some negative developments (Biro et al., 2000):

> Counteracting this trend to professionalization, however, is a militant, blue-collar union sentiment. In Ontario some police associations have openly declared that they have taken lessons from American police unions who have long been in the political arena. At the extreme is the Toronto Police Association, which has challenged the police chief on disciplinary matters, planned to endorse political candidates who supported their views on policing, hired private investigators to ensure the facts come out when police officers are accused of wrong-doing, and solicited funds from members of the public to support their efforts. . . .While most police associations have distanced themselves from these tactics, other Ontario police associations have held widely reported confidence votes on the abilities of their police chiefs. . . . (p. 15)

The appearance of a truly antagonistic approach taken by police associations is, of course, disturbing to the public and governing authorities alike. The case of the Toronto Police Association, and its campaign to generate support for its own political agenda under the presidency of Craig Bromell, has been alarming and has provoked a great deal of criticism (Gillmor, 2000). However, Toronto is not the only jurisdiction where serious labour/management friction has come to the forefront. The city of Montreal has been the setting for a great deal of union-management unrest and opposition (Forcese, 1992, p. 242). Also, in New Brunswick the Moncton Police Association passed a non-confidence motion in 1987 in respect to an extended conflict with the chief of police. Battle lines have been drawn in many jurisdictions where the police association has ceased to believe in the capacities and capabilities of its police leadership. It may amount to a crisis in modern Canadian policing (Forcese, 1992, p. 243).

COLLECTIVE BARGAINING AND ARBITRATION

Police associations in Canada operate, at the most basic level, in order to bargain with appropriate civic officials with respect to their salaries and benefits. In the case of the RCMP its elected divisional representatives deal with the federal Treasury Board over salary issues. Clearly, there is an interest in monitoring what other police services have won with regard to their salary increases and there is a great deal of "catch-up" bargaining that takes place to ensure that the collective agreement of one association is as attractive as the collective agreement of another, similar police department. In looking out for the interests of their members, police associations are primarily concerned with seeking the best financial circumstances possible. When negotiations between labour and management fail to produce an agreeable solution on these matters, arbitration typically provides that solution. As outlined by Forcese (1992):

> Most observers of labour relations favour arbitrated awards, allowing settlements to be reached (imposed in the case of binding arbitration), without job action and the associated disruption. Arbitration may also be used to find a solution where a strike is already underway. In policing, where usually the employees do not have the right to strike, arbitration awards have been the favoured resolution mechanism. Increasingly, however, arbitrators awards have been criticized by public representatives and management as excessive. (p. 245)

There is a substantial focus on police labour relations found in Part VIII of the *Police Services Act*. Issues with respect to arbitration are dealt with by the Ontario Police Arbitration Commission. This body, continued under the terms of the *Police Services Act*, and under section 131(5), has the following responsibilities:

1. Maintaining a register of arbitrators who are available for appointment under section 124.
2. Assisting arbitrators by making administrative arrangements in connection with arbitrations.
3. Fixing the fees of arbitrators appointed by the solicitor general under section 124.
4. Sponsoring the publication and distribution of information about agreements, arbitrations, and awards.
5. Sponsoring research on the subject of agreements, arbitrations, and awards.
6. Maintaining a file of agreements, arbitrations, and awards made under this Part.

STRIKES

At the furthest extreme of possible police labour action is the prospect of a strike. Because the police function is typically viewed as an essential service, police strikes are illegal and have been the cause of significant public alarm. However, several illegal strikes have occurred in Canadian policing history, and they have produced some dramatic results. As noted by Forcese (1992):

> Everywhere in Canada the years of the late 1970s and the early 1980s were periods of great labour conflict with police groups. From Victoria to St. John's, police resorted to job action, threats to strike and actual strikes. Against this background, police won very substantial salary gains. In Vancouver, police threatened their first ever strike (The Ottawa Journal, January 8, 1980), and in Quebec and Nova Scotia, police did withdraw their services. (p. 246)

Among the most radical of police associations has been the police brotherhood in Quebec, which staged a brief, illegal strike in 1976 in Montreal. There have been strikes in several Canadian jurisdictions including Sydney, Nova Scotia, in 1971; Halifax, Nova Scotia, in 1981; and Glace Bay, Nova Scotia, in 1984.

POLITICS AND LOBBYING

Canadian police have typically been removed from politics. In fact, most provincial legislation dealing with the police and local police policies prohibits officers from becoming involved in the political realm. This attitude of complete separation from the political dimension has changed in recent years. This is particularly true in Ontario, where a regulation was introduced under the *Police Services Act* dealing with the political activities of police officers. This regulation (O.Reg. 554/91) was amended in 1998 as a result of the activities of the Toronto Police Association and a desire to clarify some of the political activities that were open to police officers (see O.Reg. 89/98, amendment under the *Police Services Act*).

Recent political battles have created some interesting dilemmas within the world of police associations in Ontario, as witnessed by the withdrawal of the Ontario Provincial Police Association (OPPA) from the PAO over concerns about municipal police costing proposals. The matter of OPP "takeovers" of municipal and regional police locations under the terms of a contract with the Ontario solicitor general has created a considerable degree of animosity between the PAO and the OPPA. This is symbolic of a fundamental issue that needs to be immediately addressed by the

Credit: Denis Drever

Showing respect at the Police and Peace Officers' National Memorial Day ceremony.

provincial government as part of its overall mandate for setting provincial policy with respect to policing in Ontario.

PUBLIC RELATIONS

In working toward creating a more favourable climate for their efforts on behalf of their members, many (if not most) police associations have been engaged in carefully orchestrated efforts to improve their public image. Often this has meant that police associations have hired professional public relations and advertising consultants to assist the association in crafting an effective campaign to generate support for their membership or for some matter of policy endorsed by the association.

The national, provincial, and even local police associations have become quite sophisticated in their efforts to address concerns within the public forum. This has meant that these associations have invested large sums of money in such efforts. Clearly there is a belief that this money is well spent and operates for the greater good not only of the association but also of the public through its influence on public policy.

SPECIFIC POLICE ASSOCIATIONS IN CANADA

We will now turn to some of the major police association representative bodies in Canada. Because of the focus of this textbook, we will begin with a discussion of the Police Association of Ontario, the Ontario Provincial Police Association, and the Toronto Police Association. However, this chapter will also consider the national body, the Canadian Police Association, and its role as the umbrella organization for all police associations across Canada.

POLICE ASSOCIATION OF ONTARIO

The Police Association of Ontario was founded in 1933. The PAO is the official voice and representative body for Ontario's front-line police personnel, and provides representation, resources, and support for the province's municipal police associations. The current membership of the PAO is approximately 13 000 police and civilian members of municipal police forces.

It is relatively safe to say that the policing function during the 1930s was somewhat ill defined. Policing was guided by several different pieces of legislation, and there were unclear distinctions between police officers serving with the Ontario Provincial Police and those functioning in cities, villages, and towns. There was often considerable (if not exclusive) reliance on the quality and priorities of the local municipal government in respect to policing matters. Employment conditions were not reliable or consistent, and such things as workers' compensation or health and safety benefits were virtually unknown. Individual police officers could be dealt with in what may only be viewed as arbitrary ways. Basically, police officers as a class of workers had little collective power and few reliable employment rights and privileges.

In 1933, within this context, the Police Association of Ontario was formed. It was initially composed of first class constables in 25 different cities in Ontario who worked an average of 58.76 hours a week. During the early 1930s, it became apparent that policing standards were not adequate for meeting the needs of a modern Canadian society. In order to discuss this reality, Ontario's police leaders held a meeting on October 11, 1933, at the Royal York Hotel in Toronto. As a result of this meeting, the Police Association of Ontario came into existence. In 1944, the PAO was incorporated and, therefore, could involve itself in the collective bargaining for Ontario's police officers. This signalled an increase in the PAO's impact on government policy in Ontario. In 1945, the *Workmen's Compensation Act* began to cover employees at the municipal level of government in Ontario, and in 1946, Ontario's first *Police Act* came into existence. The PAO collaborated with the Chief Constables' Association in the establishment of the Ontario Police College, and classes began at this facility in 1963.

During the late 1950s the PAO pursued concentrated efforts in the important field of pension reform. The creation of a province-wide pension scheme for police officers had proven to be a difficult task to accomplish. In 1965, all municipal police officers not enrolled in a registered pension plan had to enroll in the Ontario Municipal Employees Retirement System, and, for the first time in the history of the police profession in Ontario, all police officers became entitled to a pension as a condition of service. By 1961, over 95 per cent of police officers in Ontario were members of the PAO.

During the 1970s one of the most controversial issues facing the PAO involved the whole concept of civilian review of police services. In fact, as recently as September 2001, the current PAO president sent detailed correspondence to the Ontario attorney general attacking the Special Investigations Unit and its director. The PAO was determined to maintain a position at the table for any discussions pertaining to amendments to the *Police Act* and sought standing as a key stakeholder in deliberations that would impact on policing policy in the province. Of critical importance to the PAO was the matter of police service amalgamations within Ontario. Between 1966 and 1981, the number of municipal police forces in Ontario had decreased from 282 to 127.

During the 1980s, the PAO was deeply involved in the process whereby the new *Police Services Act* came into existence. This legislation was given royal assent on June 28, 1990. It included a new citizen complaint process, and a new burden of proof requirement under the Code of Offences. It also introduced modifications in the legal indemnification provided to officers convicted of a criminal offence while act-ing in good faith in the performance of their duty.

Beginning in 1992 the PAO hosted its first labour conference, a feature that has continued on an annual basis to provide excellent background content for police as-sociation members, as well as for the policing community at large (PAO, 1996). These conferences are designed to critically review a broad range of police and labour re-lations topics.

In 1996, the solicitor general and minister of correctional services, the Honourable Bob Runciman, hosted a "Police Summit" designed to generate discussion and focus serious attention on issues pertinent to policing in Ontario. The PAO constituted a key stakeholder during these deliberations and participated fully in the creation of amend-ments to the *Police Services Act*. As an organization, the PAO continues to play an ac-tive and vital role in the development, design, and evaluation of policing policy in the province of Ontario.

SERVICES PROVIDED BY THE POLICE ASSOCIATION OF ONTARIO

As part of its overall purpose to "elevate the standards of the police profession, and to advance the collective interests of [its] members," the PAO offers the following key services:

- *Membership*—all rank and file municipal police officers and civilian members of municipal police forces are members of the PAO;
- *Provincial legislation*—through lobbying and representation with government principals, the PAO has made significant advances on a number of critical pieces of legislation that may impact on membership. This has included Bill 136 (Contract Arbitration), Bill 105 (*Police Services Act* amendments), and Bill 26 (Municipal Financing and Contract Arbitration);
- *Standards*—for several years the PAO has been represented on a provincial committee overseeing standards for all Ontario police services. Over the past year the PAO has been a lead stakeholder in ministry discussions concerning new standards and regulations for Ontario police services. Once approved, these standards will influence local decisions concerning a wide range of polic-ing responsibilities and issues, including staffing and resources; auxiliary police; criminal investigations; police communications; and tactical units;
- *Committees*—the PAO represents members on a variety of government com-mittees dealing with policing issues, including the Ontario Police Health and Safety Committee; Ontario Police Arbitration Commission; Ontario Municipal

Employees Retirement System; Equipment Advisory Committee; Police Learning System Advisory Committee; and SIU Consultative Committee;

- *Communication and Networking*—member associations affiliated with the PAO are routinely informed of PAO activities and developments within the police community. The PAO magazine is distributed to all PAO members in an effort to increase member awareness of issues affecting the front-line civilian member or police officer;
- *Technology and Resources*—as an organization, the PAO continues to look for means to use technology to improve efficiency and increase service levels for its members. It maintains a secure database on the Internet, providing statistical data, arbitration awards, and other information to provide easy access for local association representatives. The PAO also has a public website, which enhances its communications and increases the level of information between the PAO and members of local police associations. In addition, the PAO maintains a law library and subscriptions to a variety of related periodicals and research materials.
- *Training and Education*—the PAO provides ongoing support for member association representatives through a range of training programs, including PAO Negotiations Workshop, Ontario Police College; PAO Mediation/Arbitration Workshop, Ontario Police College; Joint *Police Services Act* Seminars, Ontario Police College; PAO Media Relations Course, Canadian Police College; PAO Effective Presentations Seminar, Ontario Police College; Annual PAO Educational Seminars, held in each region of the province; workshops on topical issues held in conjunction with PAO meetings; and specialized workshops, which have included Pay Equity, Workers' Compensation, and Human Rights;
- *Labour Relations*—through its annual labour relations conference, the PAO promotes cooperative labour/management relations; and
- *Amalgamations*—because members throughout Ontario are faced with a potential change of local police service delivery, the PAO maintains a watching brief on possible amalgamations and municipal police costing proposals. While the PAO does not advocate any particular policing model, and does not offer an opinion on a preferred delivery model, it does maintain that no member, police or civilian, should be disadvantaged as a result of a change in police service delivery.

ONTARIO PROVINCIAL POLICE ASSOCIATION

In 1963 the government of Ontario granted collective bargaining rights to the Ontario Provincial Police Association, and in 1968 their first "memorandum of understanding" was finalized (Higley, 1984).

The OPPA is the professional police labour relations organization that lobbies on behalf of the members of the OPP. It is the exclusive bargaining agent for officers within the Ontario Provincial Police up to and including the rank of sergeant major. As is noted in its Strategic Plan, the OPPA advocates and represents its membership in:

- Developing and applying the terms of the employment contract;
- Providing legal services;
- Providing support services to active and retired members, surviving spouses, and dependent children in order to enhance their quality of life; and
- Serving members in a compassionate and sensitive manner.

The OPPA has articulated a number of "key success factors" that guide its operation on behalf of its membership:

- Leadership;
- Member satisfaction;
- Values assessment;
- Financial viability;
- Employee satisfaction; and
- An effective performance management system.

TORONTO POLICE ASSOCIATION

When the Metropolitan Toronto Police Force was created in 1957, the former police associations from the following municipalities were amalgamated to form the Metropolitan Toronto Police Association: East York; Etobicoke; Forest Hill; Leaside; Long Branch; Mimico; New Toronto; North York; Scarborough; Swansea; Toronto; Weston; and York Township.

Currently, as the Toronto Police Association, this organization consists of fifteen full-time staff, nine directors, and several part-time consultants. The association maintains a detailed website and publishes a newsletter entitled *Tour of Duty Magazine*, which covers the issues and concerns of the membership.

CANADIAN POLICE ASSOCIATION

The Canadian Police Association was incorporated in 1948. It represents the national voice for approximately 30 000 police personnel across Canada. Through its 12 affiliates, membership includes police personnel serving in nearly 300 police services from Canada's smallest towns and villages to those working in our largest municipal police services.

The CPA is composed of an elected president and executive vice-president, one vice-president from each province, and a vice-president representing the CN/CP

Railway Police, the RCMP Members Association, and the First Nations Police Association respectively. The CPA staff is composed of an executive officer, a director of labour services, a communications officer, and a support staff serving in their national headquarters in Ottawa.

LEGISLATIVE ISSUES

The Canadian Police Association is acknowledged as a leading national voice for police personnel in the reform of the Canadian criminal justice system. The CPA has played a key leadership role by advancing public safety in many important areas of concern, including:

- Bill C-55, the high-risk offenders bill;
- DNA search warrants and national DNA data bank;
- Parole and sentencing reform;
- *Young Offenders Act* reform;
- Deportation of foreign criminals;
- Streamlining the *Criminal Code*;
- Criminal pursuits; and
- Organized crime.

LABOUR ISSUES

The Canadian Police Association serves as the national repository for police labour relations information. The CPA provides assistance and information in areas such as collective bargaining, employee benefits, and health and safety.

EDUCATION/AWARENESS

Twice a year the CPA holds national conferences which bring together police association leaders from across Canada to share experiences, address current issues, and develop national positions. The CPA produces annual and quarterly publications for the benefit of its members, including the nationally acclaimed *Express* magazine.

The Canadian Police Association devotes its time and resources to make a difference in many communities. By raising awareness on law enforcement and justice issues, the CPA promotes community safety. By participating in important events, such as the annual Police and Peace Officers' National Memorial Day ceremony, the CPA maintains a strong relationship between the policing community and the public. Public service is seen as a cornerstone of the organization's efforts and is demonstrated by its sponsorship and endorsement of various policing and community events, including:

- CPA Awards of Excellence;
- Cops for Cancer; and
- Kids and Cops.

In 1998, the Canadian Police Association adopted a three-year strategic business plan to focus and guide its efforts and attention to core activities. The CPA sponsors the Canadian Resource Centre for Victims of Crime, which has led the fight to restore balance to the Canadian justice system and ensure equitable treatment on behalf of victims of crime in Canada. As the national voice for all Canadian police personnel, through the representation of member labour associations, the CPA has committed itself to:

- Ensuring the welfare of Canadian police personnel by securing a safe and equitable working environment;
- Promoting the highest standards of professionalism within policing; and
- Protecting police officers and the public by advocating progressive justice reform.

The CPA represents the national centre for police labour relations, and operates to serve all member police associations representing police personnel throughout Canada. Essentially, the role of the CPA is to:

- Promote the interests of front-line police personnel and the public they serve, in the national legislative and policy fields;
- Provide a collective support network and clearinghouse for member associations to successfully improve representation and conditions for their own members in the following areas: collective bargaining, education and training, equipment, health and safety, and members' rights;
- Advocate for adequate and equitable resources for policing;
- Identify key national issues which impact its members and facilitate the resolution of these issues;
- React and respond, upon request, to local policing issues which may have national ramifications; and
- Liaise with the international policing community on issues affecting Canadian police personnel.

The core values of the CPA are listed below:

- Credibility and integrity;
- Financial accountability;
- Quality of work life; and
- Flexible and creative strategic thinking.

By acting upon these core values with consistency, the CPA strives to provide quality service through effective communications, leadership, teamwork, and responsible use of resources.

By following its core strategies the CPA seeks to achieve its ideal future vision. These core strategies are listed below:

- *Organizational effectiveness*—to ensure the CPA has the best organizational structure and systems in place to serve its members in the most effective way possible;
- *Labour relations*—to collect and share information on labour relations practices, to help improve the working conditions and wages for members;
- *Political activity*—to maximize energy and efforts at putting members' issues and concerns before the public and politicians throughout Canada;
- *Justice reform*—to lobby for and bring about justice reform on issues affecting CPA members and the Canadian public;
- *Financial stability*—to create a sustainable financial base for CPA to secure its long-term viability and stability; and
- *Planning*—to ensure CPA conducts its business in the most efficient way possible in order to achieve its strategic planning initiatives.

HISTORY OF THE POLICE MEMORIAL SERVICE

Following the murder of Ottawa rookie constable David Kirkwood, on July 11, 1977, Ottawa police officers made a vow to keep his memory alive and to honour his profound personal sacrifice. It was seen as important that the memory of other slain officers be remembered and, as a result, on Sunday, September 24, 1978, a special service and tribute were held. The site selected was Parliament Hill. The original ceremonies were limited to police and correctional officers killed, but in 1995 this approach was expanded to include all peace officers.

POLICE AND PEACE OFFICERS' NATIONAL MEMORIAL DAY

On September 24, 1998, the government of Canada officially proclaimed that the last Sunday of September would be designated as Police and Peace Officers' National Memorial Day. This offers Canadians an annual opportunity to offer formal recognition and appreciation for the dedicated service provided by police and peace officers, those who make the ultimate sacrifice in order to maintain safe communities.

On March 22, 1994, Prime Minister Jean Chrétien joined police officers and the relatives of slain officers in a solemn ceremony. The Canadian Police Association and the Canadian Association of Chiefs of Police dedicated the new Canadian Police Memorial Pavilion to those officers killed in the line of duty. The granite base of the pavilion displays the names of the fallen officers.

Honour guard at the Police and Peace Officer's Memorial.

RESOLUTIONS OF THE CANADIAN POLICE ASSOCIATION

For the year 2001, resolutions dealing with the following justice initiatives and concerns have been outlined in detail by the Canadian Police Association:

- Child pornography;
- National sex offender registry;
- Organized crime gangs;
- Victims' rights;
- Young offenders;
- DNA evidence;
- Protection for police officers;
- Correctional Service Canada;
- Health and safety of RCMP officers;
- Private security;
- Open borders;
- Impaired driving;
- Disarming of police officers;
- Penalties for murder;
- Drug enforcement;
- Injuring or endangering police animals;
- Immigration and deportation enforcement;
- Truth in sentencing;
- Arrest for parole violation;

- Accountability of the judiciary;
- Reception of the truth into evidence in criminal matters;
- Communicable disease notification in criminal matters;
- Weapons offences;
- Auto theft;
- Employee rights for RCMP officers;
- First Nations police;
- RCMP contract policing; and
- National and federal policing responsibilities.

ROYAL CANADIAN MOUNTED POLICE PAY COUNCIL

Under the *Canada Labour Code*, members of the RCMP cannot engage in collective bargaining. As a result, the RCMP Pay Council was established in May 1996 to provide a modern and efficient alternative to collective bargaining. The council was designed to resolve issues of pay and benefits in a consultative and consensual manner. It should be noted that the regulations under the *RCMP Act* provide for a Division Staff Relations Representative Program, whose purpose is to represent members with respect to staff relations matters.

MANDATE OF THE PAY COUNCIL

The mandate of the RCMP Pay Council is to make recommendations concerning the working conditions of regular members from the rank of special constable up to and including the rank of superintendent, as well as non–Special Services civilian members of the RCMP. The working conditions within the Pay Council mandate include:

- Pay and annual salary ranges;
- Various leave provisions;
- Shift differentials;
- The Senior Constable Allowance;
- Housing and transportation subsidies;
- Pensions;
- Statutory holidays;
- Public service health care plans;
- Life insurance; and
- Annual hours of work.

REPRESENTATIVES ON THE PAY COUNCIL

The Pay Council includes the following members:

- An independent chairperson;
- Two management representatives appointed by the RCMP commissioner;
- A division Staff Relations Representative member elected by caucus; and
- A compensation specialist selected by the Division Staff Relations Representatives.

POLICE SERVICES USED FOR SALARY COMPARISONS BY THE PAY COUNCIL

Historically, the compensation paid to RCMP officers of constable rank has been compared with the compensation paid to constables in several large police forces to help determine the base salary rate. These forces consist of:

- Edmonton Police Service;
- Halifax Regional Police Service;
- Montreal Urban Community Police Service;
- Ontario Provincial Police;
- Sûreté du Québec;
- Toronto Police Service;
- Vancouver Police Department; and
- Winnipeg Police Service.

COMPENSATION DETERMINATION PROCESS

Section 22(1) of the *RCMP Act* provides that the "Treasury Board shall establish the pay and allowances paid to members of the RCMP." In its Preliminary 1999 Annual Report, the Pay Council recommended that RCMP members be compensated at the average of the top three police departments in the "comparator universe," on a total compensation basis. As a result, the federal Treasury Board approved the following pay package for 2000/2001:

- 2% salary increase effective January 1, 2000
- 2.73% salary increase effective July 1, 2000
- 3% salary increase effective January 1, 2001
- shift differential increased to $1 per hour
- Senior Constable Allowance (SCA) increased to 4% for those with at least 7 years of service and passing the corporal qualifying exam. For others, the SCA remains at 2% after completing 11 years of service.
- service pay increased to $9.50 per month for each completed five-year block of service.

CONCLUSION

This chapter has provided an overview of police labour relations in Canada, with a concentration on the province of Ontario and the national body that serves the interests of police associations across the country. We have seen that the militancy of the early days of policing has given way to a more highly organized, but still aggressive, approach to collective bargaining in the area of police officer rights and privileges. It is also clear that police associations have functioned very effectively.

Furthermore, it should be clear that police associations in Canada have functioned not only to improve the overall status of police officers as employees, but also to improve the general level of public safety and order within the country. It has been a mark of the success of the police associations that they have often developed into formidable political lobby groups. Their expertise in policing matters has made them virtually indispensable stakeholders when governments have turned their attention to policing law reform and innovation.

QUESTIONS FOR CONSIDERATION AND DISCUSSION

1. Is it beneficial to have police associations?
2. Are there other means for police officers to protect their rights other than through police associations?
3. What circumstances would justify a police service going on strike?
4. What circumstances would justify police officers "working to rule"?
5. What political responsibilities or freedoms should a police officer have in Ontario? in Canada?
6. Was the True Blue campaign of the Toronto Police Association justified?
7. Should police associations be encouraged to support "law and order" candidates in municipal, provincial, or federal elections? If so, why? If not, why not?
8. What distinguishes police executive reforms from police association reforms?

RELATED ACTIVITIES

1. Review newspaper articles dealing with police strikes or other police labour actions, and consider the impact and resolution of these events.
2. Research the True Blue campaign launched by the Toronto Police Association and discuss its outcomes and the reactions of various groups, including the senior executive of the Toronto Police Service, the Toronto Police Services Board, the Toronto Municipal Council, the Ontario government, and the public at large.

3. Review available collective agreements for a local police association and discuss how the clauses and elements contained within that agreement were arrived at in discussions with police management.
4. Examine Part VIII (Labour Relations) of the *Police Services Act* and discuss the issues that this part raises with respect to collective bargaining and police officers in Ontario.
5. Review current, or back, issues of police association newsletters and magazines. Discuss issues and controversies that have been addressed by these representative bodies on behalf of their members.
6. Research the controversy over the whole issue of civilian oversight of policing in Ontario and discuss the arguments for and against the existing cycle of police oversight in place in Ontario.
7. Research the advent of the Special Investigations Unit (SIU) in Ontario and summarize the key points of opposition to this oversight body.

REFERENCES

Anderson, John C. (1980). "The employer-employee relationship in police labour relations. In Downie, Bryan M. and Richard L. Jackson (eds.) *Conflict and cooperation in police labour relations*. Ottawa: Supply and Services Canada.

Arthurs, H.W. (1971). *Collective bargaining by public employees in Canada: five models*. Ann Arbor, Mich.: Institute of Labor and Industrial Relations.

Biro, Fred, Peter Campbell, Paul McKenna, and Tonita Murray (2000). *Police executives under pressure: a study and discussion of the issues*. Ottawa: Canadian Association of Chiefs of Police. (Police Futures Group; study series no. 3)

Bisaillon, Guy and Andre Durivage (1991). "A viewpoint on Quebec police labour relations." *Canadian Police College Journal*, Vol. 15, no. 2, pp. 118–136.

Downie, Bryan M. and Richard L. Jackson (eds.) (1980). *Conflict and cooperation in police labour relations*. Ottawa: Supply and Services Canada.

Fisher, E.G. and Henry Starek (1980). "Police bargaining in Canada: private sector bargaining, compulsory arbitration and mediation-arbitration in Vancouver." In Downie, Bryan M. and Richard L. Jackson (eds.) *Conflict and cooperation in police labour relations*. Ottawa: Supply and Services Canada.

Forcese, Dennis (1980). "Police unionism: employee-management relations in Canadian police forces." *Canadian Police College Journal*, Vol. 4, no. 2, pp. 79–129.

Forcese, Dennis (1992). *Policing Canadian society*. Scarborough, Ont.: Prentice-Hall Canada.

Gillmor, Don (2000). "The thick blue line." *Toronto Life* (October), Vol. 34, no. 16, pp. 126–130.

Goldsmith, Andrew J. (1986). The impact of police collective bargaining upon municipal police management in Ontario, 1973-1984: socio-legal analysis: a thesis submitted in conforming with the requirements for the degree of Doctor of Juridical Science, University of Toronto.

Grant, A. (1975). "The control of police behaviour." In Tarnopolsky, W.S. (ed.) *Some civil liberties issues of the seventies*. Downsview, Ont.: Osgoode Hall Law School, York University.

Grant, A. (1977). "Towards a model for police management training." *Criminal Law Quarterly*, Vol. 19.

Harvie, R.A. and P.E. Lawson (1978). "Occupational implications of police collective bargaining." *Police Studies*, Vol. 1.

Higley, Dahn D. (1984). *O.P.P.: the history of the Ontario Provincial Police Force*. Toronto: Queen's Printer.

Jackson, R.L. (1979). "Police labour relations in Canada." *Canadian Police College Journal*, Vol. 3, no. 1, pp. 16–43.

Juris, Hervey A. and Peter Feuille (1973). *Police unionism*. Lexington: D.C. Heath & Co.

LaFleche, Grant and Cheryl Stepan (2000). "Trend shows police unions getting what they want," *National Post*, January 17, 2000.

Marquis, Greg (1993). *Policing Canada's century: a history of the Canadian Association of Chiefs of Police*. Toronto: University of Toronto Press and the Osgoode Society.

Martin, Dianne L. (2000). "True Blue: is it right for a police association to do what is wrong for an individual officer to do?" *Emond-Montgomery's Academic Publications Bulletin*, Vol. 1, no. 2 (March). Toronto: Emond-Montgomery.

Perrier, D.C. (1979). "Is policing a profession?" *Canadian Journal of Criminology*, Vol. 21.

Police Association of Ontario (1996). *Police employment in 1996: seeking the common sense solution: two day conference, February 26-27, 1996*. Mississauga: Police Association of Ontario.

Quinn, Jennifer and John Duncanson (2000). "Police chiefs feel heat of union," *Toronto Star*, January 14, 2000.

Reiner, Robert (1978). *The blue collar worker: a sociological study of police unionism*. London: Cambridge University Press.

Royal Canadian Mounted Police Pay Council (1999). *Royal Canadian Mounted Police Pay Council final 1999 annual report*. Ottawa: Royal Canadian Mounted Police.

Swan, Kenneth (1980). "Interest arbitration of non-economic issues in police bargaining." In Downie, B.M. and R.L. Jackson (eds.) *Conflict and cooperation in police labour relations*. Ottawa: Department of Supply and Services Canada.

WEBLINKS

www.rnca.ca Visit the site of the Royal Newfoundland Constabulary Association to read about its history, learn about its executive, and see what types of community activities it is involved with.

www.bcfedpolice.com The British Columbia Federation of Police Officers' website offers a link to each of the police departments in British Columbia, as well as to BC RCMP detachments. You can also access the *Thin Blue Line*, which is the federation's official magazine.

www.abbotsfordpoliceunion.org The Abbotsford Police Association's site allows viewers to familiarize themselves with association news, the APA executive, the Abbotsford police, and the city of Abbotsford.

 www.yrpa.on.ca The York Regional Police Association's website introduces users to itself, provides information about its activities within the community, and has links to York Region resources.

 www.mppa.bc.ca The website of the BC Mounted Police Professional Association features information on its constitution, its executive, relevant news, and other resources.

 wwww.oppa.on.ca Along with basic information about the Ontario Provincial Police Association, this website offers links to the Officer Down Memorial Page, the National Fallen Firefighters Foundation, and the National EMS Memorial Service page.

 www.pao.on.ca Visit the website of the Police Association of Ontario to find out how Ontario's police officers can benefit from membership. You can access the association's magazine, looking through past articles to enhance your knowledge of policing in Ontario.

 www.cpa-acp.ca The Canadian Police Association's website offers links to the latest news for Canadian police officers, as well as sections dedicated to justice reform, media releases, and publications. There are also pages describing the awards and distinctions that Canadian officers can be nominated for.

 http://labour.hrdc-drhc.gc.ca/psait_spila/lmric_irlc//irlc_html/ Police(1)(e).htm On this website you will find a list of the statutes governing Canadian police officers on the matter of collective bargaining, divided by province and territory.

 www.sover.net/~tmartin/International.htm Knowing the laws of one's own province and country is crucial to effective law enforcement, but it is also useful to know about the rules, regulations, and community programs of other cities and countries in the world. Visit the international Law Enforcement website to find information on law enforcement issues and news on a larger scale.

www.rcmp-grc.gc.ca/html/paycouncil-e.htm The RCMP Pay Council was established in 1996 because RCMP officers, under the Canada Labour Code, cannot engage in collective bargaining. This website outlines the history of the RCMP Pay Council and provides province-specific information for users. Learn how being a Royal Canadian Mounted Police Officer differs from being a provincial or town police officer.

CHAPTER FIVE

FIRST NATIONS

POLICING IN CANADA

LEARNING OBJECTIVES

1. Define First Nations policing in Canada.
2. Identify key elements relevant to the growth and development of First Nations policing in Canada.
3. Distinguish between on-reserve and off-reserve First Nations policing issues.
4. List the goals of First Nations self-policing initiatives.
5. List several First Nations police organizations in Canada.

INTRODUCTION

This chapter will provide a brief overview of some topics relevant to First Nations policing in Canada. This is an area that has been changing dramatically over the last decade, and while it is not possible to cover this area of study thoroughly, it is hoped that the information provided will allow students to pursue broader studies in this important area of Canadian policing.

We will look at some of the basic demographic data currently available on Canada's First Nations peoples and consider some of the different groupings that will have an impact on future directions in First Nations policing. There is a distinction made between off-reserve and on-reserve First Nations peoples and their respective policing needs and expectations. The central question of a separate First Nations justice system will be addressed in this chapter, and various First Nations policing programs currently in place within the RCMP and the OPP will be considered as examples of the significant transformation of policing.

FIRST NATIONS DEMOGRAPHICS IN CANADA

Statistics Canada is an excellent source of information on the demographic profile of Canada's First Nations peoples. In the 1996 Census, it was determined that approximately 3 per cent of Canada's total population, or 799 010 individuals, reported themselves to be North American Indian, Métis, or Inuit. This finding has been further broken down by Statistics Canada to reveal that two-thirds of this Aboriginal population (i.e., 554 000 people) identified themselves as North American Indian, one-quarter (about 210 000) identified themselves as Métis, and 41 000 identified themselves as Inuit. Table 5.1 provides an overview of the Canadian Aboriginal population.

TABLE 5.1

ABORIGINAL IDENTITY POPULATIONS 1996

	Total Population	Total Aboriginal Population	Aboriginal Population as % of Total Population
Canada	28 528 125	799 010	2.8
Newfoundland	547 160	14 205	2.6
P.E.I.	132 855	950	0.7
Nova Scotia	899 970	12 380	1.4
New Brunswick	729 630	10 250	1.4
Quebec	7 045 080	71 415	1.0
Ontario	10 642 790	141 525	1.3
Manitoba	1 100 295	128 685	11.7
Saskatchewan	976 615	111 245	11.4
Alberta	2 669 195	122 840	4.6
British Columbia	3 689 755	139 655	3.8
Yukon	30 655	6 175	20.1
N.W.T.	64 120	39 690	61.9

Source: Statistics Canada (1998). *The Daily*, Tuesday, January 13.

As a result of the 1996 Census, it has also been determined that one in five Aboriginal people lives in seven census metropolitan areas (CMAs) in Canada. These figures are further detailed in Table 5.2.

It is also relevant, from a criminal justice perspective, that the average age of the Aboriginal population in Canada is 10 years younger than the rest of the population.

TABLE 5.2

ABORIGINAL IDENTITY POPULATION IN SELECTED CENSUS METROPOLITAN AREAS 1996

	Total Population	Total Aboriginal Population	Aboriginal Population as % of Total Population
Toronto	4 232 905	16 100	0.4
Winnipeg	660 055	45 750	6.9
Regina	191 480	13 605	7.1
Saskatoon	216 445	16 160	7.5
Calgary[a]	815 985	15 200	1.9
Edmonton	854 230	32 825	3.8
Vancouver	1 813 935	31 140	1.7

[a]These CMAs contain, within their boundaries, Indian reserves, which were incompletely enumerated during the 1996 Census. Consequently, their counts of North American Indians are affected by this incomplete enumeration.

Note: Respondents identified themselves as belonging to at least one Aboriginal group: North American Indian, Métis, or Inuit.

Source: Statistics Canada (1998). *The Daily*, Tuesday, January 13.

In 1996, the average age for an Aboriginal person was 25.5 years, while in the rest of Canada, that average age was 35.4 (Statistics Canada, 1998).

POLICING OFF RESERVES

As the number of Aboriginal people living off reserves is quite significant, it is important that there be strategies and guidelines in place for addressing the policing needs of this population. Several task forces and public inquiries have gone to great lengths to emphasize this reality, and it has been an important topic of study by the federal solicitor general, whose mandate includes Aboriginal policing issues.

Controversy has arisen in cities like Saskatoon, where the municipal police have had to respond to serious charges of racism in their handling of Aboriginal persons. Particular events in 2001 brought the police department to the attention of Amnesty International and created a crisis for the chief of police and the Saskatoon Board of Police Commissioners. The controversy arose after the bodies of Rodney Naistus and Lawrence Wegner were discovered near a Hydro station outside of the Saskatoon

Credit: Mike Weaver, Media Relations, Kingston Police

The *Criminal Code* guides policing across Canada.

city limits on January 29 and February 3 respectively. Neither of these Aboriginal men had jackets on, and they had frozen to death. It was alleged that these men had been taken out by Saskatoon police officers and told to walk back to town. In September 2001, two Saskatoon police constables were convicted of unlawful confinement for taking another local Aboriginal man, Darrell Night, out to the edge of the city and abandoning him. These officers were fired by the chief of police for their actions (*StarPhoenix*, September 22, 2001).

Approaches to community-based and problem-solving policing are required to address the needs of an Aboriginal community living off reserves. There has to be a special emphasis on crime prevention initiatives aimed at Aboriginal youth, who represent a growing proportion of the off-reserve population.

The federal solicitor general has provided substantial support for innovative and progressive initiatives that will work toward better policing services for this community. Within the federal solicitor general's office, the Aboriginal Police Directorate has been established to administer First Nations policing. The mission of this directorate is:

- To contribute to the development, implementation and maintenance of First Nations and Inuit policing services that are professional, effective, efficient and responsive to the unique needs of these communities; and

- To support the Solicitor General and the Deputy Solicitor General in the exercise of their respective responsibilities regarding First Nations policing and law enforcement.

POLICING ON RESERVES

In June 1991, the federal government announced its First Nations policing policy. This policy was designed to increase the control of Canada's First Nations over the policing services they receive. First Nations could elect to develop and administer their own law enforcement services, or they could have these services delivered by First Nations officers who would function within existing police departments.

The RCMP First Nations Community Policing Service represents a contingent of First Nations police officers working within the structure of the RCMP. It is intended that the RCMP First Nations Community Police Service, in consultation with Aboriginal community leaders, will develop arrangements that will suit the specific policing needs of the community (Royal Canadian Mounted Police. Community, Contract and Aboriginal Policing Services, 1998).

The Ontario Provincial Police also administers a First Nations Policing program, as a result of a tripartite agreement involving the federal government, the province of Ontario, four recognized First Nations Associations of Ontario, and other communities. The OPP undertakes measures to ensure the staffing, equipping, and the coordination of training for First Nations constables. The OPP provides a liaison with those First Nations who maintain stand-alone police services.

The goal of the OPP First Nations Policing program is as follows:

> To support the transition to self policing of First Nations Territories in Ontario. In concert with the First Nations Communities and consistent with their aspirations and government policy, this Program is committed to building bridges between cultures in order to facilitate the transition. (Source: OPP website at www.gov.on.ca/opp)

ABORIGINAL POLICE SERVICES

Several Aboriginal police services have been developed in Canada. There are many examples of where individual First Nations bands have created their own law enforcement organization. Often these departments have been developed in collaboration with non-Aboriginal police services; however, their mandate is to provide a stand-alone service within their community. While this textbook will not examine individual Aboriginal police services in Canada, it will note the formation of the First Nations Chiefs of Police Association and consider some of its goals.

The First Nations Chiefs of Police Association was formed in 1992 and has the following objectives (1992):

1. To encourage and develop the establishment of First Nations Police Services to provide adequate services to First Nations Communities and Territories throughout Canada.
2. To encourage, promote and foster adequate and meaningful training programs to meet the needs of First Nations Police Services.
3. To encourage and establish liaison among all Canadian First Nations Police Services and other First Nations Government and organizations.
4. To encourage high efficiency in First Nations Law Enforcement.
5. To promote and maintain high standards of ethics, integrity, honour and conduct in the profession of First Nations Policing, taking into account traditional values and First Nations traditional law.
6. To foster and encourage Policing and other programs to ensure the safety and security of residents of First Nations Communities and Territories.

FUTURE DEVELOPMENTS IN ABORIGINAL POLICING

In their detailed study of self-administered First Nations policing conducted on behalf of the federal solicitor general, Clairmont and Murphy (2000) make the following observations:

> FN [First Nations] communities and political leaders may have to reconsider the resource implications of trying to achieve round-the-clock, highly visible, conventional policing which is also proactive, culturally sensitive and community-based. Under existing funding arrangements, where the police budget is separately provided through tripartite negotiations, FNs do not have to balance off policing against other competing services but, quite rationally, can focus on seeing policing issues in terms demanding more resources. It would appear that there has to be, in other words, on the part of government and FNs, much more collaboration in setting forth a more focused, directed policing model or models that can be reasonably implemented with committed resources that are not profoundly inconsistent with general Canadian patterns. Perhaps the time is now ripe for concerned parties to discuss, reach some consensus on, and plan for the vision(s) they have of FN policing. (p. 47)

CONCLUSION

This chapter has taken a fairly cursory look at the issues impacting on First Nations policing in Canada. We have considered some of the recent demographic information on First Nations peoples and the reality that many of their members reside in large urban areas. There is a double challenge of ensuring that the diverse needs of First Nations communities be met both on reserve and off reserve. It is clear that there are distinctive challenges posed by both elements. It is also clear that the federal government, in partnership with the provinces, territories, and the First Nations and Aboriginal peoples themselves, is working toward a revised vision of what policing will be in the future.

QUESTIONS FOR CONSIDERATION AND DISCUSSION

1. Why are First Nations peoples seeking to control their own policing services?
2. Are there differences between Aboriginal and non-Aboriginal approaches to policing and law enforcement?
3. Why are First Nations peoples overrepresented in our correctional system in Canada?
4. How have the federal solicitor general and the RCMP adapted their approach to First Nations policing in Canada?
5. What role does the Ontario Provincial Police play in the area of First Nations policing?
6. How would First Nations communities determine if they wished to have their own stand-alone police service, or contract for policing services through the RCMP?
7. How would off-reserve policing of First Nations peoples differ from on-reserve policing?
8. What measures should be taken to ensure that First Nations police services are not unduly influenced by their local band council?
9. What role do organizations like the Assembly of First Nations, the Métis National Council, the Native Women's Association of Canada, and the Inuit Tapirisat play with respect to First Nations policing?

RELATED ACTIVITIES

1. Review issues of the *First Nations Policing Update*, published under the auspices of the federal solicitor general, and select topics that are relevant for classroom discussion or independent research projects.
2. Review one of the task force reports or public inquiries dealing with First Nations justice in Canada. What is the status of the recommendations made by the task force of inquiry? Have there been positive developments? How have recommendations been implemented?
3. Locate a First Nations police service within your jurisdiction and request background information on that organization and its policies and procedures.

REFERENCES

Alberta. Department of the Attorney General (1991). *Justice on trial: Task Force on the criminal justice system and its impact on the Indians and Métis people of Alberta*. Edmonton: Department of the Attorney General.

Benson, Garry F. (1991). *Developing crime prevention strategies in aboriginal communities*. Ottawa: Solicitor General of Canada.

Canada. Task Force on Policing on Reserves (1973). *Task force on policing on reserves: report*. Ottawa: Department of Indian Affairs and Northern Development.

Clairmont, D. and C.J. Murphy (2000). *Self-administered First Nations' policing: an overview of organizational and management issues*. Ottawa: Solicitor General Canada.

Clark, Scott (1989). *The Mi'kmaq and criminal justice in Nova Scotia: a research study*. Halifax: Royal Commission on the Donald J. Marshall Jr. Prosecution.

Depew, R. (1986). *Native policing in Canada: a review of current issues*. Ottawa: Ministry of the Solicitor General.

Dubé, Yves (1995). *Policing options available to First Nations in Canada: working paper*. Ottawa: Solicitor General Canada.

First Nations Chiefs of Police Association (1992). "Objectives and Bylaws" [online]. [Cited November 25, 2001.] <http://www.soonet.ca/fncpa/objective.htm>.

Griffiths, Curt T. (1994). "Policing aboriginal peoples." In Macleod, R.C. and David Schneiderman (eds.) *Police powers in Canada: the evolution and practice of authority*. Toronto: University of Toronto Press.

Hamilton, A.C. and C.M. Sinclair (1991). *The justice system and aboriginal people: report of the Aboriginal justice inquiry Manitoba*. Winnipeg: Queen's Printer.

Jobson, Keith B. (1993). *First Nations police services: legal issues*. Victoria, B.C.: Ministry of the Attorney General.

Landau, Tammy (1996). *A model protocol for evaluations of First Nations police services*. Ottawa: Solicitor General Canada, Aboriginal Policing Directorate.

LaPrairie, Carol (1991). *Justice for the Cree: communities, crime and order*. Quebec: Cree Regional Authority.

LaPrairie, Carol et al. (1991). *Justice for the Cree: final report*. James Bay, Que.: Cree Regional Authority.

Law Reform Commission of Canada (1991). *Aboriginal peoples and criminal justice*. Ottawa: The Commission.

Loree, Don (1985). *Policing native communities*. Ottawa: Canadian Police College.

Murphy, C.J. and D. Clairmont (1996). *First Nations police officers survey*. Ottawa: Solicitor General Canada.

Ontario. Race Relations and Policing Task Force (1989). *The report of the Race Relations and Policing Task Force*. Toronto: Ontario Ministry of the Solicitor General.

Ontario. Race Relations and Policing Task Force (1992). *The report of the Race Relations and Policing Task Force*. Toronto: Ontario Ministry of the Solicitor General.

Royal Canadian Mounted Police. Community, Contract and Aboriginal Policing Services (1998). *RCMP First Nations community policing service*. Ottawa: RCMP.

Samuelson, Les (1993). *Aboriginal policing issues: a comparison of Canada and Australia*. Ottawa: Solicitor General Canada.

Saunders, Lauren (1995). *First Nations police governing authorities operations and procedures: a "how to" manual*. Ottawa: Solicitor General Canada.

Stenning, Philip C. (1996). *Police governance in First Nations in Ontario*. Toronto: Centre of Criminology, University of Toronto.

Taylor, Keith (1998). *Crime prevention for First Nations communities: self evaluation manual*. Ottawa: Solicitor General Canada.

WEBLINKS

 www.sgc.gc.ca The website of the federal solicitor general contains a wealth of information on the First Nations policing program, including many of the research studies and background papers cited in the References section of this chapter.

 www.aboriginalcanada.gc.ca The Aboriginal Canada Portal, sponsored by Indian and Northern Affairs Canada, is an important Internet gateway providing access to an enormous amount of data and information about Canada's Aboriginal peoples. There is a "Justice and Policing" section within the Aboriginal Canada Portal that hosts several valuable links to relevant government information.

 www.rcmp-ccaps.com The RCMP maintains a website for its Community, Contract and Aboriginal Policing Services directorate. This website includes details relevant to its Aboriginal policing program.

 www.apscops.org Visit the Anishinabek Police Service website to see how First Nations policing has become an integral part of Canadian (Ontarian) society over the past 10 years, and to see the subtle differences in approach, as with this police service's mission statement and patch design information.

 www.bloodtribepolice.com The Blood Tribe Police Service website's history and service pages highlight the way in which First Nations policing has made a resurgence in Canadian society, specifically in Alberta.

 www.stp.bc.ca The Stl'atl'imx Tribal Police service, located in British Columbia, was created in 1986 by the Lillooet Council Band. See how this service's history and philosophy of policing compare to other First Nations police services, as well as provincial police and the RCMP.

 www.sgc.gc.ca/whoweare/aboriginal/efnpp.htm The First Nations Policing Policy, introduced by the federal government in 1991, is key to providing effective police service to First Nations communities. This website offers a detailed explanation of the policy, including access to relevant publications and newsletters.

www.globalinfo2000.com/gb/services/cfnpa Formed in 1998, the Canadian First Nations Police Association supports and enhances First Nations policing in Canada. Its website offers access to related labour issues and the organization's history newsletters.

 www.ainc-inac.gc.ca/gs/dem_e.html The Indian and Northern Affairs Canada website provides detailed information on First Nations issues from strategies for Aboriginal businesses to demographics to culture and history. This background information will enhance your understanding of First Nations policing in Canada.

 www.explorenorth.com/library/weekly/aa111999.htm Murray Lundberg's article (The Social Construction of Crime in Canadian Aboriginal Societies) discusses the ways in which location and time define crime in a particular society, specifically Canadian Aboriginal society.

 www.turtleisland.org/news/news-justice.htm A police officer must be aware of the sensitive issues associated with the law enforcement profession, especially to ensure that human rights are not violated. The Turtle Island Native Network's website contains accounts of possible police misconduct and brutality against Native people for your consideration, as well as the United Nations Guidelines for Indigenous Peoples.

CHAPTER SIX

POLICE USE OF FORCE

LEARNING OBJECTIVES

1. Define police use of force as applied in Canada.
2. List examples of lethal and less-than-lethal (or non-lethal) force available to police officers in Canada.
3. Distinguish between reasonable use of force and excessive use of force by police.
4. Outline the national use of force framework approved for use in Canada.
5. Identify sources of relevant case and statute law dealing with police use of force in Canada.

INTRODUCTION

This chapter will address some issues related to the police use of force. This will include considerations of lethal and less-than-lethal force that can be applied by police officers in pursuit of their duties. We will also review the national use of force framework recently approved by the Canadian Association of Chiefs of Police and examine relevant legislation that touches on this topic. It is one of the profound ironies of modern policing that officers must become highly skilled in the use of a wide range of different types of force, including lethal force, and yet the sincere hope is that these officers will never have to resort to the application of force in the conduct of their duties.

This chapter will consider the different force options available to officers. We will also consider the decisions that must be made in order to arrive at a reasonable, and ultimately defensible, decision on the part of officers to use force, recognizing that they will be under a great deal of pressure and stress.

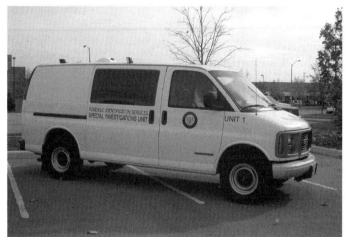

Credit: Special Investigations Unit

The SIU is deployed throughout the province of Ontario.

THE NATIONAL USE OF FORCE FRAMEWORK

The Canadian Association of Chiefs of Police (CACP) has recently approved a national use of force framework (Canadian Association of Chiefs of Police. Human Resources Committee, 2001b). This detailed framework has been released for use by police agencies across Canada and was in development for several years. For example, in 1993, the Ontario Police College, in Aylmer, worked with representatives from major police services in Ontario to develop an effective use of force training model. This particular model was introduced during court proceedings and has proven to be a valuable mechanism for educating the courts and the public on the police use of force. The Human Resources Committee of the CACP provides some background on the construction of use of force schemes (Canadian Association of Chiefs of Police. Human Resources Committee, 2001a):

> Graphics or models that describe use of force by police officers first began to appear in the 1970's in the United States. These early models depicted a rather rigid, linear-progressive [sic] process, giving the impression that the officer must exhaust all efforts at one level prior to being allowed to consider alternative options, a kind of stair step process. A frequent complaint lodged against these early models was that they did not accurately reflect the dynamic nature of potentially violent situations in which the entire range of officer, subject, and force options must be constantly assessed throughout the course of the interaction. (p. 14)

In 1999, the CACP supported a proposal to hold a conference at the Ontario Police College that would work toward the formulation of a nationally recognized use of force model. The conference was held April 8–10, 1999, and was attended by 65 police use of force specialists from across Canada. The agreed-upon model contains detailed descriptions of each component of the framework, and incorporates the most solid theory, practice, and research available pertaining to police use of force. The final product was presented to the CACP board of directors for approval. In November 2000, the board endorsed the use of force framework. The model incorporates a colour graphic that is intended to enhance its presentation and clarity (Canadian Association of Chiefs of Police. Human Resources Committee, 2001a), and furthermore:

> As an aid to training, the framework promotes continuous critical assessment and evaluation of each situation and assists officers to understand and make use of a variety of force options to respond to potentially violent situations. (p. 16)

The CACP use of force model is outlined in Figure 6.1.

FIGURE 6.1

NATIONAL USE OF FORCE FRAMEWORK

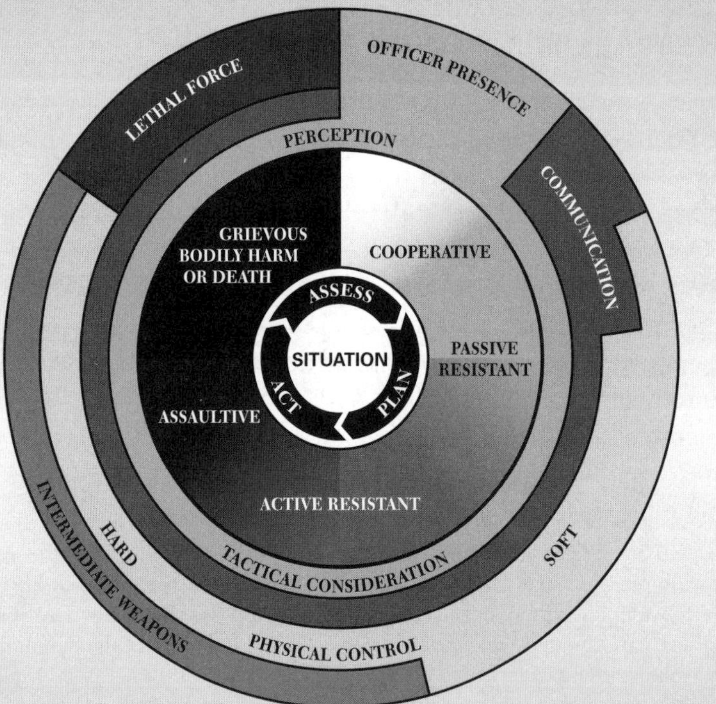

The officer continuously assesses the situation and acts in a reasonable manner to ensure officer and public safety.

Source: CACP Newsletter, vol. 20, no. 1 & 2 (Spring/ Summer), p. 12. Used by permission of the Canadian Association of Chiefs of Police.

THE POLICE USE OF FORCE CONTINUUM

Before the introduction of the CACP's national use of force framework, much effort had been invested in understanding the issue of police use of force. There is nothing that serves to alienate the police organizations from the public they serve more dramatically than the perception that their officers are prone to the use of excessive force in the exercise of their legal authority. We are all familiar with comprehensive media coverage of police shootings or instances of alleged police brutality. Such events immediately focus intense scrutiny on police officers and their departments. They can quickly become the source of the deepest, most damaging criticism levelled against individual police officers, their supervisors, or their governing authorities. Accordingly, considerable thought must be given to the introduction of reasonable and responsible limits around police use of force and the application of available alternatives to lethal force (Geller and Toch, 1995).

It is important to remember that police officers in Canada are *required* to use reasonable force in the protection of themselves and the public. This requirement derives from section 27 of the *Criminal Code*, a statute that applies to all police officers in Canada:

> Every one is justified in using as much force as is reasonably necessary
>
> (a) to prevent the commission of an offence
>   (i)   for which, if it were committed, the person who committed it might be arrested without warrant, and
>   (ii) that would be likely to cause immediate and serious injury to the person or property of anyone, or
> (b) to prevent anything being done that, on reasonable grounds, he believes would, if it were done, be an offence mentioned in paragraph (a).

There are additional protections for peace officers when they are carrying out their lawful duties, as outlined in subsection 25(4) of the *Criminal Code*:

> A peace officer, and every person lawfully assisting the peace officer, is justified in using force that is intended or is likely to cause death or grievous bodily harm to a person to be arrested, if
>
> (a) the peace officer is proceeding lawfully to arrest, with or without warrant, the person to be arrested;
> (b) the offence for which the person is to be arrested is one for which that person may be arrested without warrant;
> (c) the person to be arrested takes flight to avoid arrest;
> (d) the peace officer or other person using the force believes on reasonable grounds that the force is necessary for the purpose of protecting the peace officer, the person lawfully assisting the peace officer or any other person from imminent or future death or grievous bodily harm; and
> (e) the flight cannot be prevented by reasonable means in a less violent manner.

While the *Criminal Code* authorizes the use of necessary force for lawful purposes, officers are also accountable to federal and applicable provincial laws in the exercise of that authority. There are frequently detailed policies and procedures in place within each individual police service for the specific rules and regulations that pertain to the application of federal and provincial statutes regarding use of force.

As a result of a recent comprehensive study, Geller and Toch (1995) have developed a table that clearly indicates where the attention of a police department should be concentrated in matters relating to use of force. This presentation makes important distinctions between various levels of force and places the use of force into a range of reasonableness that can assist the organization, and the officers involved, in making appropriate responses. Table 6.1 outlines the details of that presentation.

TABLE 6.1

EXTENT OF DEPARTMENTAL ATTENTION TO DIFFERENT TYPES OF USE OF FORCE ISSUES

Amount of Force Used	Quality of Officer's Decision		
	A Unreasonable	B Reasonable	C Highly Skilled
1 No force (or very minor force) used	Unreasonable Restraint	Justifiable Restraint	Commendable Restraint
2 Moderate force used (isolated incident)	Abuse of Force	Justifiable Use of Force	Commendable Use of Force
3 Serious force used (isolated incident)	Abuse of Force	Justifiable Use of Force	Commendable Use of Force
4 Moderate to Serious force used Frequently	Abuse of Force (Violence-prone officer &/or dept. problems)	Justifiable Use of Force (guidance, retraining, dept. changes)	Commendable Use of Force (Dept. strategic &/or tactical changes)

KEY: Shaded cells represent police conduct that typically receives attention from most police departments. The behaviour noted in unshaded cells receives far less consideration.

Source: Excerpted from Geller, William A. And Hans Toch. (eds.) *And justice for all: understanding and controlling police abuse of force.* © 1995, Police Executive Research Forum, Washington, D.C. Used with permission.

In Ontario considerable attention has been paid to the creation of a use of force continuum to guide police officers, police executives, and the public with regard to the proportionate application of coercive force by police officers (Ontario. Ministry of the Solicitor General. Policing Services Division, 1992). The use of force continuum developed in Ontario would ultimately form the foundation for the national use of force framework discussed above. However, it served to highlight the complications that relate to the decision-making process each officer must confront in a wide variety of operational situations. In developing guidelines to shape local policy with respect to police use of force, individual police services must take into consideration:

1. *Firearms*—including the type of weapon that will be authorized for use (revolver versus semi-automatic), the type of ammunition that will be authorized for use (hollow-point versus semi-wadcutter), holsters, and reloaders, grip adapters or other adaptations of the issued weapon, and many other equipment issues that pertain to weapon selection;

2. *Reporting systems*—including the requirements to report any discharge of the firearm, or other weapons including gas, chemical, or aerosol weapons, training and requalification records, and other related reports;

3. *Training and requalification*—including the provision of an established cycle of instruction for all officers and the maintenance of full records on officers' performance during any training program. Topics may include legal requirements regarding the use of force, demonstration of judgment, review of safety considerations, theoretical framework for use of force legislation and policies, practical exercises designed to test and enhance proficiency, including handgun retention techniques; and

4. *Use of force options*—including a configuration that permits officers to move along a continuum which emphasizes that the *least* amount of force should be employed in any given circumstance, while also recognizing that a situation may require the selection of the most extreme options in order to protect the officer or the public. This configuration includes the following elements:

   - Officer presence;
   - Tactical communications;
   - Empty-hand techniques—including soft (controlling techniques) and hard (empty hand strikes);
   - Impact weapons—including soft (weapon augmented restraint) and hard (defensive impact strikes);
   - Aerosol weapons; and
   - Firearms.

The *Police Services Act* in Ontario contains a regulation dealing with equipment and the use of force (see Regulation 926, R.R.O. 1990, amended to O.Reg. 361/95). This regulation sets out the technical specifications for handguns to be used by police officers in Ontario. Table 6.2 presents those technical specifications.

TABLE 6.2

TECHNICAL SPECIFICATIONS FOR HANDGUNS

ITEM	SPECIFICATION
1.	Weapon type i. Semi-automatic pistol, A. That requires a single consistent trigger pressure of not less than 8 pounds and not more than 13 pounds to discharge the weapon on each shot, and B. all the safety features of which are housed within or are a part of the trigger system.
2.	Calibre i. 9 x 19 mm (3.5") ii. .40 S & W
3.	Barrel length i. Minimum 90 mm (3.5") ii. Maximum 130 mm (5")
4.	Finish i. Corrosion-resistant ii. Non-reflective
5.	Sights i. Fixed Metal ii. Self-luminating
6.	Operation i. The slide remains locked fully open after the last round in the magazine is fired. ii. The pistol has an external device that allows the slide to be manually locked open. iii. The pistol has drop safety protection capable of preventing an accidental discharge when dropped from a height of four feet.

Source: Reprinted by permission of Queen's Printer for Ontario, 2002. © Queen's Printer for Ontario, 2002.

Before a member of a police service can be issued with a firearm, the OPP commissioner, or the chief of police, must be satisfied that the member has completed required training. Accordingly, the regulation also outlines the training in the use of force required under the regulation and the retraining and requalification in use of force and use of firearms. The training program must include the following elements:

- Legal requirements;
- The exercise of judgment;
- Safety;
- Theories relating to the use of force; and
- Practical proficiency.

There is also a standardized Use of Force Report that must be completed, in accordance with section 14.5(1) of the regulation, whenever the member:

(a) draws a handgun in the presence of a member of the public, excluding a member of the police force while on duty, or discharges a firearm;
(b) uses a weapon other than a firearm on another person; or
(c) uses physical force on another person that results in an injury requiring medical attention.

Figure 6.2 reproduces the approved form for the Use of Force Report.

In the context of use of force training, there has been a great deal of effort invested in the production of training scenarios that use simulators and other advanced educational technologies to provide realistic exercises for officers. These tools have their advocates because they incorporate decision-making patterns that can be linked with operational and administrative policies within the police department. They can also be structured to generate reports on individual officer performance in these simulations in order to ensure that complete records are maintained and that any necessary remedial training can be scheduled quickly. However, Fyfe (1995) highlights the significant limitations of too heavy a reliance on even the most sophisticated electronic use of force training scenarios. Beyond the warning to resist the temptations of too much gadgetry, Fyfe recommends that broad use of force training policies cannot substitute for local proficiency enhancement that is tailored to immediate circumstances:

> The need to fit training to the needs of individual communities is yet another reason why police agencies should regard commercial or other out-of-house training as a complement to their own training effort. No commercial vendor who directs training at a wide market can possibly anticipate or address the characteristics of individual jurisdictions. And despite their greater proximity to the departments they serve, it is extremely difficult for state or regional academies to do so. Assuring that training is congruent with community demographics requires real *hands-on* effort by local police departments. (p. 171) [emphasis in original]

FIGURE 6.2

Form 1

Police Services Act

USE OF FORCE REPORT

(Check more than one box in each section, where appropriate)

Police Service   Location Code (if applicable)

Part A

Date (day/month/year)   Time Incident Commenced (24 hr)   Time Incident Terminated (24 hr)

☐ Individual Report   Length Of Service (years completed)   Rank   ☐ Team Report   Type of Team   # of Police Officers Involved

Type of Assignment
- ☐ General Patrol
- ☐ Foot Patrol
- ☐ Traffic
- ☐ Investigation
- ☐ Drugs
- ☐ Off-duty
- ☐ Other (specify)

Type of Incident
- ☐ Robbery
- ☐ Break and Enter
- ☐ Domestic Disturbance
- ☐ Other Disturbance
- ☐ Traffic
- ☐ Suspicious Person
- ☐ Serious Injury
- ☐ Homicide
- ☐ Weapons Call
- ☐ Alarm
- ☐ Other (specify)

Police Presence At Time Of Incident
- ☐ Alone
- ☐ Police Assisted (specify#)

Attire
- ☐ Uniform ☐ Civilian Clothes

Number of Subject(s) Involved In Incident
- ☐ One ☐ Two ☐ Three ☐ Other (specify #)

Type Of Force Used (Includes all options used during incident & rank in sequence of use)

	Was Force Effective? Yes No
Firearm - discharged	☐ ☐
Firearm - pointed at person	☐ ☐
Handgun - drawn	☐ ☐
Aerosol Weapon	☐ ☐
Impact Weapon - Hard	☐ ☐
Impact Weapon - Soft	☐ ☐
Empty Hand Techniques - Hard	☐ ☐
Empty Hand Techniques - Soft	☐ ☐
Other (specify)	☐ ☐

Reason For Use Of Force
- ☐ Protect Self
- ☐ Protect Public
- ☐ Effect Arrest
- ☐ Prevent Commission of Offence
- ☐ Prevent Escape
- ☐ Accidental
- ☐ Destroy an Animal
- ☐ Other (specify)

Alternative Strategies Used (If Applicable)
- ☐ Verbal Interaction ☐ Cover
- ☐ Concealment ☐ Other (specify)

Type of Firearm Used (If Applicable)   **No. of Rounds Discharged** (If Applicable)
- ☐ Revolver
- ☐ Semi-automatic
- ☐ Rifle
- ☐ Shotgun
- ☐ Other (specify)

Distance (Between you & subject at the time the decision was made to use force)
- ☐ Less than 2 metres
- ☐ 2 to 3 metres
- ☐ 3 to 5 metres
- ☐ 5 to 7 metres
- ☐ 7 to 10 metres
- ☐ Greater than 10 metres

Weapons Carried By Subject(s)   1 2 3
- ☐ ☐ ☐ Unknown
- ☐ ☐ ☐ None
- ☐ ☐ ☐ Revolver
- ☐ ☐ ☐ Semi-automatic
- ☐ ☐ ☐ Rifle
- ☐ ☐ ☐ Shotgun
- ☐ ☐ ☐ Knife/Edged Weapon
- ☐ ☐ ☐ Baseball Bat/Club
- ☐ ☐ ☐ Other (specify)

Location Of Subject's Weapon (At time decision was made to use force)   1 2 3
- ☐ ☐ ☐ In-hand
- ☐ ☐ ☐ At hand
- ☐ ☐ ☐ Concealed on person

Number of Rounds Fired By Subject(s) (If Applicable)

Total Number: _____

Location Of Incident

Outdoors
- ☐ Roadway
- ☐ Laneway
- ☐ Yard
- ☐ Park
- ☐ Rural
- ☐ Motor Vehicle
- ☐ Other (specify)

Indoors
Private Property
- ☐ House
- ☐ Apartment
- ☐ Halfway

Public Property
- ☐ Financial Institution
- ☐ Commercial Site
- ☐ Public Institution
- ☐ Other (specify)

Weather Conditions
- ☐ Clear
- ☐ Sunny
- ☐ Cloudy
- ☐ Rain
- ☐ Snow/sleet
- ☐ Fog
- ☐ Other (specify)

Lighting Conditions
- ☐ Daylight
- ☐ Dusk
- ☐ Dark
- ☐ Good Artificial Light
- ☐ Poor Artificial Light
- ☐ Other (specify)

Person Injured	Medical Attention Required Yes No		Nature of Injuries Minor Serious Fatal Unknown
1. Self	☐ ☐		☐ ☐ ☐ ☐
2. Other Police Officer	☐ ☐		☐ ☐ ☐ ☐
3. Subject	☐ ☐		☐ ☐ ☐ ☐
4. Third Party	☐ ☐		☐ ☐ ☐ ☐

Narrative: (if no occurrence report) - Do not include personal names or information.

If more space is required please continue on back of form.

Reviewed by Supervisor ☐ Yes ☐ No   Reviewed by Training Analyst ☐ Yes ☐ No   Recommended Post Traumatic Incident Counselling ☐ Yes ☐ No   Recommended Other Training ☐ Yes ☐ No   Date (day/month/year)

Part B

Officer Involved (name, rank & badge #)

Date of last use of force refresher training   Would you like to participate in an interview with a training sergeant/analyst to discuss this incident and/or use of force training? ☐ Yes ☐ No

Additional training recommended by: ☐ training analyst ☐ supervisor   Type of training recommended:

O. Reg. 751/92, s 2

Source: Reprinted by permission of Queen's Printer for Ontario, 2002. © Queen's Printer for Ontario, 2002.

Credit: Mike Weaver, Media Relations, Kingston Police

Kingston Police officer honours the Ontario Police Memorial at Queen's Park.

CONCLUSION

This chapter has considered some of the elements that must be considered when police officers confront the decision to use differing levels of force. Canada has arrived at a shared conceptual framework dealing with police use of force through the efforts of the Canadian Association of Chiefs of Police and several use of force experts across the country.

It is important to emphasize that police departments train their officers in the full range of use of force options in order to support their officers' legal responsibility to protect the public and themselves, and to prevent harm. It is unreasonable to assume that police officers will always be able to resolve every situation without resorting to some type of force and it is also unreasonable to expect officers to protect our freedom, our lives, our peace, and our property without having the wherewithal to act decisively when circumstances dictate. The challenge for the individual police officer is to be capable and competent not only in the various use of force options but, more importantly, to be highly skilled in the decision-making processes that will test their proficiency across the full spectrum of use of force options.

QUESTIONS FOR CONSIDERATION AND DISCUSSION

1. Why is a linear approach to police use of force not seen as being adequate?
2. What different forms of force are available to Canadian police departments?
3. What are the key components of the new national use of force framework adopted by the Canadian Association of Chiefs of Police?
4. Is it reasonable to expect police officers to submit a complete report every time they use their firearm in the presence of a member of the public?
5. To what extent should a police department be responsible for ensuring that its officers have training in the use of force options?
6. How important is the psychological screening of police recruit candidates with respect to use of force issues?
7. What is the best method for reviewing police officer decision-making in instances where force (both lethal and non-lethal) has been used?

RELATED ACTIVITIES

1. Review the use of force policies and procedures of a local police service. Discuss these policies and procedures in the context of the *Criminal Code* and any provincial legislation (e.g., the *Police Services Act* and its regulations) as it relates to the use of force.
2. Examine the local, or national, media for coverage of incidents of police use of force. This may be particularly valuable in cases where there have been allegations of excessive use of force by the police.
3. Locate articles and essays in the police literature that deal with different types of police weapons and discuss them in the context of the use of force legislation that you have examined in class.
4. Review recent sources of case law (e.g., *Canadian Criminal Cases*) for decisions dealing with police use of force. Discuss the facts surrounding selected cases and explore the issues raised in the case in the context of this chapter.

REFERENCES

Adams, K. (1995). "Measuring the prevalence of police abuse of force." In Geller, William A. and Hans Toch (eds.) *And justice for all: understanding and controlling police abuse of force.* Washington, D.C.: Police Executive Research Forum.

Alpert, Geoffrey P. and L.A. Fridell (1992). *Police vehicles and firearms: instruments of deadly force.* Prospect Heights, Ill.: Waveland.

Alpert, Geoffrey P. and Roger G. Dunham (1995). *Police use of deadly force: a statistical analysis of the Metro-Dade Police Department.* Washington, D.C.: Police Executive Research Forum.

Alpert, Geoffrey P. and Roger G. Dunham (1997). *The force factor: measuring police use of force relative to suspect resistance*. Washington, D.C.: Police Executive Research Forum.

Alpert, Geoffrey P. and Michael Smith (1999). "Police use-of-force data: where we are and where we should be going." *Police Quarterly*, Vol. 2, no. 1 (March), pp. 57–78.

Alpert, Geoffrey P. et al. (2000). *Police pursuits: what we know*. Washington, D.C.: Police Executive Research Forum.

Binder, A., P. Scharf and R. Galvin (1982). *Use of deadly force by police officers: final report*. Washington, D.C.: National Institute of Justice.

Canadian Association of Chiefs of Police. Human Resources Committee (2001a). *Canadian Association of Chiefs of Police 2001 Annual Report: CACP presents a national use of force framework*. Ottawa: Canadian Association of Chiefs of Police.

Canadian Association of Chiefs of Police. Human Resources Committee (2001b). "National use of force framework approved by CACP executive." *CACP Newsletter*, Vol. 20, no. 1&2 (Spring/Summer), p. 12.

Chappell, Duncan and Linda P. Graham (1985). *Police use of deadly force: Canadian perspectives*. Toronto: Centre of Criminology, University of Toronto.

Condon, Richard J. (1985). *Police use of deadly force in New York State*. Albany: Division of Criminal Justice Services.

Cox, Terry, Jerry S. Faughn, and William M. Nixon (1985). "Police use of metal flashlights as weapons: an analysis of relevant problems." *Journal of Police Science and Administration*, Vol. 13, No. 3, pp. 244–250.

Crawford, Charles and Ronald Burns (1998). "Predictors of the police use of force." *Police Quarterly*, Vol. 1, no. 4, pp. 41–64.

Desmedt, J.C. (1984). "Use of force paradigm for law enforcement." *Journal of Police Science and Administration*, Vol. 12, pp. 170–76.

Forcese, Dennis P. (1992). *Policing Canadian society*. Scarborough: Prentice-Hall Canada.

Fyfe, James J. (1978). "Shots fired: an examination of New York City police firearms discharges." Ph.D. dissertation, State University of New York at Albany.

Fyfe, James J. (1988). "Police use of deadly force: research and reform." *Justice Quarterly*, Vol. 5, no. 2, pp. 165–205.

Fyfe, James J. (1995). "Training to reduce police-civilian violence." In Geller, William A. and Hans Toch (eds.) *And justice for all: understanding and controlling police abuse of force*. Washington, D.C.: Police Executive Research Forum.

Geller, William A. and Michael Scott (1992). *Deadly force: what we know: a practitioner's desk reference on police-involved shootings*. Washington, D.C.: Police Executive Research Forum.

Geller, William A. and Hans Toch (eds.) (1995). *And justice for all: understanding and controlling police abuse of force*. Washington, D.C.: Police Executive Research Forum.

Hontz, Thomas A. (1999). "Justifying the deadly force response." *Police Quarterly*, Vol. 2, no. 4 (December), pp. 462–476.

Jacobs, D. and R. O'Brien (1998). "The determinants of deadly force: a structural analysis of police violence." *American Journal of Sociology*, Vol. 103, no. 4, pp. 837–62.

MacDonald, Victor, M.A. Martin and A.J. Richardson (1985). "Physical and verbal excesses in policing." *Canadian Police College Journal*, Vol. 9, no. 3, pp. 295–341.

McEwen, Tom (1996). *National data collection on police use of force*. Washington, D.C.: U.S. Dept. of Justice, Office of Justice Programs, jointly published with the National Institute of Justice.

McKenna, Paul F. (1998). *Foundations of policing in Canada*. Scarborough: Prentice Hall Canada.

Milton, C.H. et al. (1977). *Police use of deadly force*. Washington, D.C.: Police Foundation.

Ontario. Ministry of the Solicitor General. Policing Services Division (1992). *Policing standards manual for the Province of Ontario*. Toronto: The Ministry.

Pugliese, David (1998). "SWAT you're dead." *Saturday Night*, Vol. 113, no. 3 (April), pp. 40–49.

Sheehan, Robert and Gary W. Cordner (1995). *Police administration*. 3rd ed. Cincinnati, Ohio: Anderson Publishing.

Smith, Michael (1999). "Police pursuits: the legal and policy implications." *Police Quarterly*, Vol. 2, no. 3 (September), pp. 261–282.

Tonry, Michael and Norval Morris (eds.) (1992). *Modern policing*. Chicago, Ill.: University of Chicago Press.

U.S. Department of Justice. Community Relations Services (1999). *Police use of excessive force: a conciliation handbook for the police and the community*. Washington, D.C.: U.S. Dept. of Justice, Community Relations Service.

WEBLINKS

 www.icpsr.umich.edu   The Inter-University Consortium for Political and Social Research (ICPSR) at the University of Michigan was established in 1962 as a focus for social science research. The ICPSR contains a number of databases holding valuable information relevant to studies done in the United States pertaining to police use of force.

 www.ncjrs.org/pdffiles1/nij/176330-1.pdf Although this text focuses on policing in Canada, it is useful for Canadian officers to consider issues that affect them from other perspectives. This site features the U.S. Department of Justice's research report on the use of force by police.

 http://dps.psafety.unc.edu/divisionpages/ Police/Use%20of%20Force%20Report.htm The University of North Carolina at Chapel Hill's Department of Public Safety has put its use of force report on the Internet.

www.cpc-cpp.gc.ca/ecasesums.asp It is important for citizens who feel that they have been mistreated by a police officer be able to voice their concerns. The Commission for Public Complaints Against the RCMP website provides citizens with information on how to make a complaint and the process that will ensue. Relevant to this chapter is the page of case summaries on use of force complaints.

 www.theiacp.org/profassist/useofforce.htm The International Association of Chiefs of Police website features information on the National Police Use of Force Database Project that, although recently discontinued, provides insight for officers concerned about the use of force.

CHAPTER SEVEN

OFFICER SAFETY, STRESS, AND WORK-PLACE PROTECTION

LEARNING OBJECTIVES

1. Define officer safety as applied in Canada.
2. List sources of stress for police officers in Canada.
3. Define post-traumatic stress disorder.
4. Describe key developments in the area of officer safety.
5. Identify key elements in the area of workplace protection as related to policing in Canada.

INTRODUCTION

This chapter will consider aspects of policing that relate to officer safety, stress, and workplace protection. Because policing is an occupation that has considerable personal risk associated with it, there is a legitimate concern for the physical, psychological, and emotional protection of all officers. Because police officers have a legislated responsibility to prevent serious criminal offences and apprehend criminals, it is reasonable that every precaution will be taken to ensure their safety. This chapter will consider the elements of officer safety, including the kinds of training and equipment that have been developed for this purpose. Also, this chapter will look at the whole issue of stress, the impact that it has on police officers, and the means that have been developed to manage stress. We will look at specific topics such as shift work and its potential to contribute to officer stress, as well as post-traumatic stress as a particularly difficult element of police work. We will look at the concerns about workplace health and safety that are peculiar to policing and will consider some of the remedies that have been developed, often as a result of the efforts of police associations as they work to promote the welfare of their members.

This chapter will also make reference to the growing literature available on the various topics treated in this section. It is expected that teachers and students will avail themselves of this wealth of supplementary information to extend and deepen their own understanding of the important issues of police officer safety, stress, and workplace safety.

POLICE OFFICER SAFETY

Police officer safety refers to the range of practices, procedures, policies, and products that are designed to ensure that individual officers are protected in the pursuit of their lawful duties. Officer safety includes such considerations as training and re-qualification in the various pieces of equipment that police officers use to do their jobs, such as firearms, police vehicles, batons, handcuffs, capsicum or other sprays, and body armour. It also includes having officers well prepared in first aid and CPR. Many of these aspects also benefit the public; however, they serve immediately to safeguard officers while they are engaged in the often dangerous work of policing.

We have seen in Chapter 4 that police associations have operated on behalf of their members to arrive at collective agreements that advance their financial conditions. Police associations are also very active in pursuit of practices that support officer safety. An extremely good example of this can be found in the large-scale transition from the older style of police service revolver (often referred to as a "wheel" gun) to the more modern semi-automatic weapon. The Police Association of Ontario was deeply involved in a lobbying effort to convince police administrators that this change was essential for officer safety. The matter was seen as a health and safety issue, with the argument being made that the .38 calibre revolvers were ineffective against the powerful weapons being used by criminals in Canada. The revolver typically issued to police officers in Canada had been essentially the same since the turn of the 20th century. A great deal of research was conducted on the semi-automatic pistol, and in the 1990s the *Police Services Act* in Ontario was amended to allow police departments to issue approved models of semi-automatic weapons. A related struggle, eventually resolved in 1995, involved an effort to secure permission from the government for the use of hollow-point ammunition, the style of ammunition recommended by manufacturers and ballistics experts for semi-automatic weapons.

It is undeniable that policing is a difficult occupation. The potential for danger is always present for front-line officers, and they frequently have to deal with people in extreme situations. There is frequently serious injury or even death involved with matters confronted during "routine" patrol. Officers must handle all of these circumstances in an orderly, professional, objective, and rigorous manner, all the while acting to preserve the safety of themselves and the public.

Credit: Ontario Provincial Police

Modern equipment and technology support officer safety.

STRESS IN POLICING

Research has provided a great deal of assistance in drawing attention to the problems associated with stress in policing (Finn and Tomz, 1997). While it is a given that stress will impact on every human being, regardless of his or her occupation, the potential for dangerously high levels of stress among police personnel is considerable (Selye, 1974). Fortunately, several clinical and experimental studies of stress have generated a number of techniques and methods for dealing with the negative effects of stress (Finn and Tomz, 1997). Also, we are constantly learning more about controlling sources of stress in ways that will minimize their worst effects. Increasingly, progressive police organizations are making important investments in the resources that are necessary for these techniques and methods to be introduced in meaningful ways for the benefit of officers.

Anderson, Swenson, and Clay (1995) have identified some of the main sources of stress for police:

- Discretionary power;
- Death—including police shootings, mutilating accidents, suicides, murders, natural deaths;
- Injury—to self and/or others;
- Personal failure;
- Dangerous situations;
- Officer misconduct;

- Supervision;
- Handling disturbances;
- Judicial system;
- Outside criticism and scrutiny;
- Special assignments (e.g., undercover operations); and
- Changes in working conditions.

Added to the many operational sources of stress, which have always been a characteristic of the occupation of policing, are the stressful influences of profound and extensive organizational change, now so common in Canadian policing. The radical and fundamental transformation of the processes and structures of policing can have a powerfully stressful impact on officers who are resistant to such change and are not convinced of its value or necessity.

Beginning in the 1960s, police organizations worked with psychologists, largely to develop methods for screening applicants for recruitment. This new form of collaboration resulted from recommendations made in the U.S. following serious urban riots in 1968 (Reiser, 1972; Reese, 1987). The initial purpose for this partnership eventually grew to include some of the trained psychologists' other clinical skills which were also adaptable to police work, including:

- Critical incident response to police shootings;
- Hostage-taking and/or barricaded person negotiation skills;
- Criminal profiling;
- Forensic hypnosis; and
- Stress management and wellness training.

In addition to the professional expertise provided by psychologists, many police organizations in Canada have introduced peer counselling and support programs, which have been highly effective. Also known as employee assistance programs (EAP), such initiatives are useful in reducing absenteeism, increasing productivity, decreasing the number of grievances and disciplinary actions, and generally raising morale within the department (Anderson, Swenson, and Clay, 1995).

Frequently, training programs are designed to provide officers with the appropriate skills to undertake the functions of a peer counsellor. These individuals are then able to offer assistance following a traumatic incident, or to deal with a range of other stress-related matters that may be affecting officers. This approach allows the police service to provide qualified support to its members without provoking the officers' tendency to mistrust "outsiders," who are perceived as not understanding the circumstances of the police officer's experience.

THE PHYSIOLOGY OF STRESS

There are physiological changes that occur within the human body when one is confronted with stressful situations. Accordingly, it is useful to know about these changes in order to monitor the progression and severity of one's reactions to stress. It is also useful to be able to recognize the symptoms in others and to employ stress management techniques to reduce those symptoms. Anderson, Swenson, and Clay (1995) enumerate some of the signs and symptoms of stress in Table 7.1.

TABLE 7.1

SIGNS AND SYMPTOMS OF STRESS

Activation of the sympathetic nervous system produces the following:
Heart rate increase
Blood pressure increase
Large muscle groups tense
Adrenaline rush
Increased blood sugar
Hypervigilance
Pupils dilate
Increased hearing acuity
Increased blood clotting
Increased metabolism
Blood flow increases to heart, lungs, and large muscles
Perspiration, especially to palms
Digestive secretions slow
Dry mouth due to saliva decrease
Bowel activity decreases
Extremities become cool
Sphincter tightens
More white blood cells enter the bloodstream
Cholesterol remains in the blood longer
Dilation of the lung passages and increased respiration

Source: Adapted from Anderson, Swenson, and Clay (1995, p. 37).

Also relevant in this context is an understanding of Hans Selye's general adaptation syndrome. Selye (1974) studied three stages of reaction to sources of stress, all of which are pertinent to the work of police officers. The first stage is alarm and may be characterized by slower thinking and poor coordination. Typically, this stage does not last very long and it is succeeded by the second stage: resistance. Here, if the stress continues, a person's senses, strength, and focus are enhanced and brought into play for the fight or flight response. This stage can often provide individuals with exceptional strength as the body responds to an emergency. The last stage is exhaustion. If a person fails to recover from the stress, they will suffer exhaustion, collapse, or acute physical or psychological harm. Again, as in the alarm stage, concentration and clear thinking may be impaired.

CONTRADICTORY DEMANDS OF POLICING

The nature of policing is such that it makes some contradictory demands on officers. As a public service that is geared toward crime prevention, law enforcement, assistance to victims, emergency response, and public order maintenance, policing clearly requires radically different approaches to suit a whole host of circumstances. Dealing with victims will require one set of skills, while dealing with the criminal element will call for an entirely different set of skills. Police officers must also be able to deal with many other categories of people as they conduct their operations. They must be able to work independently, yet within a context that has an extremely high level of group cohesion. They must be able to show considerable empathy to certain groups of people, yet they must also demonstrate a firm resolve in the face of law-breakers, who will often attempt to appeal to an officer's sense of leniency. A police officer must be able to deal with long stretches of patrol duty where absolutely nothing happens, yet be able to instantaneously react when a crisis or emergency occurs requiring their expertise. While constantly being witness to the very worst aspects of human existence, an officer is still expected to maintain a positive outlook and treat all people with dignity and respect.

Police officers typically have a certain degree of autonomy and discretion on the job. However, police organizations remain highly structured. In spite of much talk about officer "empowerment," officers remain guided by substantial guidelines, policies, and procedures. While each officer can make decisions on who and when to arrest, that officer is still subject to considerable supervision, and her or his daily routines are fixed within a fairly rigid chain of command.

SHIFT WORK

It is clear that the demands of shift work take their toll on a police officer's well-being. There has been considerable research on this aspect of the job and the importance of working to reduce police fatigue. Bryan Vila (2000) has produced a recent study that takes a critical look at this question. He notes:

> At times, patrol work is very challenging, physically and emotionally. Other times, it is excru-
> ciatingly boring. Both boredom and the physically and emotionally challenging nature of patrol

work contribute to the fatigue officers experience. One can think of the effects of these occupational stressors as providing a baseline level of fatigue for patrol officers. In other words, policing can be a tough job, and some of its challenges are unavoidable. These challenges often can't be—or shouldn't be—avoided. From an administrative and preventive standpoint, what's important is that we identify sources of fatigue that *are* potentially controllable. (pp. 21–22) [emphasis in the original]

Shift work can create some difficulties in the social realm for police officers. Baxter (1978) determined that, in the U.S., fully 30 per cent of police divorces were largely attributable to the stress of the job, including the complications relating to shift work. It can pose problems in the basic management of family schedules and may mean that shift workers do not enjoy many of the normal activities that occur during the daylight hours when they are getting their rest.

Police organizations must be alert to the administrative considerations that will mitigate the negative impacts of shift work. This may include the use of forward rotations (i.e., day to afternoon, to evening shifts) rather than backward rotations (i.e., evening, to afternoon to day shifts), which have been found to be less stressful for the officer. Also, it has been determined that fixed, or permanent, schedules are somewhat easier for people to adjust to than rotating shift schedules (Jamal, 1981). Finally, police organizations should be diligent in preparing new officers for the rigours of shift work. There is much to be gained by acknowledging the impact of shift work and helping new recruits learn about preventative measures and coping mechanisms that more experienced officers have developed.

POST-TRAUMATIC STRESS DISORDER

Post-traumatic stress is an area that has received a great deal of attention in the last few decades. Finn and Tomz (1997, p. 207) define post-traumatic stress disorder as "an anxiety disorder that can result from exposure to short-term severe stress, or the long-term buildup of repetitive and prolonged milder stress."

Emotional reactions may occur not only in the context of a police officer's personal exposure to danger or injury, but also from dealing with victims who are fatally wounded or seriously injured. Not everyone reacts in the same way to traumatic events; however, most officers will have some form of post-traumatic response when confronted with a shooting incident in which someone is killed (Solomon, 1988). Individual officers will deal with such events in a variety of ways. In Table 7.2, Anderson, Swenson, and Clay (1995) list the factors that will influence those reactions.

In many instances, it will be necessary for officers who have been involved in on-duty shooting situations to receive professional psychological counselling. The im-

TABLE 7.2

FACTORS THAT INFLUENCE AN OFFICER'S REACTIONS TO A SHOOTING

- Mental preparation for the confrontation
- Recent events influencing the officer's sense of vulnerability
- Amount of control the officer has over the situation
- Degree of personal threat to the officer
- The duration of the event
- Degree to which the officer feels the shooting is justified
- Support from other officers
- Support from administration and the community
- Age and sex of the deceased

Source: Excerpted from Anderson, Swenson, and Clay (1995, p. 103).

pact of such events may be devastating, and police organizations have recognized the need to offer such support for officers who have experienced such critical incidents. The International Association of Chiefs of Police (IACP) has developed administrative guidelines that are designed for handling this type of occurrence, as well as a model policy for post-shooting incident procedures. These items have been included as Appendices A and B in this textbook.

STRESS MANAGEMENT: METHODS AND TECHNIQUES

Due to the nature of policing in Canada, it is inevitable that officers will encounter highly stressful situations. Unlike other occupations where such events may be rare, policing brings police officers into contact with traumatic, violent, and possibly deadly events. Therefore, it is essential that police officers become well-versed in methods and techniques for coping with stress.

Taking time to relax, enjoying good nutrition, and getting regular sleep and exercise are essential ingredients in dealing with stress. Having a strong network of support in the form of family and friends will also provide stability for officers who are dealing with stressful situations as part of their job. Often police officers pursue hobbies that allow them to relax on their own. There is much satisfaction to be gained in completing a hands-on project or by having constant sources of mental stimulation from ongoing learning in areas outside of policing.

In Table 7.3, Anderson, Swenson, and Clay (1995) offer a range of stress management techniques that are categorized in the context of a number of preferred learning styles.

TABLE 7.3

STRESS MANAGEMENT TECHNIQUES

Preferred Modality	Techniques
Visual	Guided imagery Photography Biofeedback (visual) Healing imagery Visual fixation Cognitive rehearsal with imagery
Auditory	Autogenic training Counting down Positive self-talk Music Biofeedback (auditory) Singing/Chanting
Kinesthetic	Progressive muscle relaxation Breathing Yoga/Tai Chi Exercise Massage/Whirlpool

Source: Adapted from Anderson, Swenson, and Clay (1995, p. 224).

DEVELOPING SUPPORT SYSTEMS

It is not useful to struggle alone with the effects of stress, regardless of whether that stress occurs on the job or in one's personal life. Too often, police officers have attempted to grapple with serious problems on their own, without support from their colleagues, their supervisors, or professional counsellors. This is beginning to change, and many police organizations have fully developed stress programs in place to assist their officers in dealing with job-related stress (Finn and Tomz, 1997). Dealing with painful situations is a common part of a police officer's job, and there must be a whole

Credit: Denis Drever

Canadian Police Memorial Pavilion.

system of supports available to help officers deal with their own emotions and feelings if they are to continue being effective employees.

In many instances, police associations in Canada have been deeply involved in the development of peer counselling or employee assistance programs geared to helping their members. One example may be found in the work of the Ontario Provincial Police Association, which offers an Employee Assistance Program (EAP). This is a voluntary and confidential counselling service that is conducted outside the workplace and offers assistance in the following areas:

- Family and marital relationships;
- Anxiety and stress;
- Alcoholism and drug dependency;
- Personal and emotional difficulties;
- Grief and bereavement issues;
- Child and adolescent concerns;
- Legal and financial information; and
- Childcare and eldercare information.

This EAP is available 24 hours a day, 365 days a year, and there are services available in both English and French. This is a highly commendable service offered to police officers and members of their immediate family and represents a progressive approach to stress management in Canadian policing.

WORKPLACE PROTECTION

It is the employer's obligation to provide its members with a safe and secure work environment. This, of course, poses an enormous challenge to modern Canadian police departments. It may be possible to prepare the police headquarters and the various satellite offices in a manner consistent with the highest standards of workplace safety. It may also be possible to ensure that police officers are provided with the most up-to-date equipment and that their vehicles and telecommunications systems are both safe and secure. However, the front-line police officer's "workplace" often includes the most dangerous neighbourhoods in town, where criminal occurrences take place against a backdrop of poverty and turmoil. How is it possible to ensure that officers will be safe in such environments?

Police administrators and police associations have often worked together to develop policies and procedures that will maximize officer safety in all these settings. Clearly there is a need for workplace safety in a conventional sense. Therefore, many joint management/association health and safety committees have been formed to monitor the workplace.

CONCLUSION

This chapter has examined some of the important aspects of officer safety, including the area of stress. There has been much emphasis placed on the methods for managing and reducing stress for police officers. Some attention has been paid to the concept of post-traumatic stress disorder and the means for handling this condition. It is clear that policing will always hold dangers for front-line officers. Thus, it is essential that police organizations do what they can to ensure that their members have a clear understanding of the methods and techniques for dealing with stress, as well as providing professional supports to sustain them when they require assistance in dealing with the enormous pressures of this occupation.

Also, we have considered workplace protection and how it impacts on the effectiveness of police officers as they conduct their lawful duties.

QUESTIONS FOR CONSIDERATION AND DISCUSSION

1. What are some of the signs of stress?
2. What are the pros and cons of an eight-hour shift rotation? a ten-hour shift rotation? a twelve-hour shift rotation?
3. How could shift work be altered to lessen its stressful effects on police officers?

4. What are some useful coping mechanisms for dealing with the effects of shift work?
5. Are there any possible ethical concerns related to confidential counselling for police officers suffering from alcoholism or drug dependency?

RELATED ACTIVITIES

1. Review a peer counselling or employee assistance program offered by a local police service and determine if it would meet the needs of officers suffering from work-related stress.
2. Locate available post-shooting incident procedures or policies available from a local police service and evaluate their contents. Do they provide clear support for officers?
3. Examine the training provided by a local police service in the related areas of stress management or peer counselling.

REFERENCES

Aaron, Jeffrey D.K. (2000). "Stress and coping in police officers." *Police Quarterly*, Vol. 3, no. 4 (December), pp. 438–450.

Adams, Ronald J., Thomas M. McTernan, and Charles Remsberg (1980). *Street survival: tactics for armed encounters*. Northbrook, Ill.: Calibre Press.

Adams, Thomas F. (1998). *Police field operations*. 4th ed. Upper Saddle River, N.J.: Prentice Hall.

Alkus, S. and C. Padesky (1983). "Special problems of police officers: stress-related issues and intervention." *Counseling Psychologist*, Vol. 11, no. 2, pp. 55–64.

Anderson, Wayne, David Swenson, and Daniel Clay (1995). *Stress management for law enforcement officers*. Englewood Cliffs, N.J.: Prentice Hall.

Anson, R.H. and M.E. Bloom (1988). "Police stress in an occupational context." *Journal of Police Science and Administration*, Vol. 16, pp. 229–235.

Ayres, R.M. (1990). *Preventing law enforcement stress: the organization's role*. Washington, D.C.: U.S. Dept. of Justice, Bureau of Justice Assistance.

Baxter, D. (1978). "Coping with police stress." *Trooper*, Vol. 3, no. 4, pp. 68, 69, 71, 73.

Blau, T. (1994). *Psychological services for law enforcement*. New York: John Wiley & Sons.

Finn, Peter and Julie Esselman Tomz (1997). *Developing a law enforcement stress program for officers and their families*. Washington, D.C.: U.S. Dept. of Justice, Office of Justice Programs, National Institute of Justice.

Forcese, Dennis P. (1992). *Policing Canadian society*. Scarborough: Prentice-Hall Canada.

Frederick, C.J. (1986). "Post-traumatic stress responses to victims of violent crime: information for law enforcement officials." In Reese, James T. and Harvey A. Goldstein (eds.) *Psychological services for law enforcement*. Washington, D.C.: Government Printing Office.

Glensor, Ronald W., Kenneth J. Peak, and Larry K. Gaines (1999). *Police supervision*. Boston: McGraw-Hill College.

Goolkasian, G.A., R.W. Geddes, and W. DeJong (1985). *Coping with police stress*. Washington, D.C.: U.S. Dept. of Justice, National Institute of Justice.

Hilgren, J.S., R. Bond, and S. Jones (1976). "Primary stressors in police administration and law enforcement." *Journal of Police Science and Administration*, Vol. 4, pp. 445–449.

Jamal, M. (1981). "Shift work related to job attitudes, social participation, and withdrawal behavior: a study of nurses and industrial workers." *Personnel Psychology*, Vol. 34, pp. 535–548.

Meagher, M.S. and N.A. Yeates (1986). "Choosing a career in policing: a comparison of male and female perceptions." *Journal of Police Science and Administration*, Vol. 14, pp. 320–327.

Nordlicht, S. (1979). "Effects of stress on the police officer and family." *New York State Journal of Medicine*, Vol. 79, pp. 400–401.

Reese, J.T. (1987). *A history of police psychological services*. Washington, D.C.: U.S. Dept. of Justice.

Reese, J.T. and H.A. Goldstein (eds.) (1986). *Psychological services for law enforcement*. Washington, D.C.: U.S. Dept. of Justice, Federal Bureau of Investigation.

Reese, J.T., J.M. Horn, and C. Dunning (eds.) (1991). *Critical incidents in policing*. Revised. Washington, D.C.: U.S. Dept. of Justice, Federal Bureau of Investigation.

Reiser, A.J. (1972). *The police department psychologist*. Springfield, Ill.: Charles C. Thomas.

Reiser, M. and S.P. Geiger (1984). "Police officer as victim." *Professional Psychology: Research and Practice*, Vol. 15, pp. 315–323.

Remsberg, Charles (1986). *The tactical edge: surviving high-risk patrol*. Northbrook, Ill.: Calibre Press.

Rosa, R.R., M.J. Colligan, and P. Lewis (1989). "Extended workdays: effects of 8-hour and 12-hour rotating shift schedules on performance, subjective alertness, sleep patterns, and psychosocial variables." *Work and Stress*, Vol. 3, no. 1, pp. 21–32.

Royal Canadian Mounted Police. External Review Committee (1990?). *Employee assistance programs: philosophy, theory and practice*. Ottawa: Royal Canadian Mounted Police External Review Committee. (Discussion paper; no. 5).

Royal Canadian Mounted Police. External Review Committee (1992). *Occupational health and safety: an employer perspective*. Ottawa: Royal Canadian Mounted Police External Review Committee.

Sarason, I.G. et al. (1979). "Helping police officers to cope with stress: a cognitive-behavioral approach." *American Journal of Community Psychology*, Vol. 7, pp. 593–603.

Scrivener, Ellen M. (1994). *The role of police psychology in controlling excessive force*. Washington, D.C.: U.S. Dept. of Justice, National Institute of Justice.

Scrivener, E. and M. Kurke (eds.) (1995). *Police psychology into the 21st century*. Hillsdale, N.J.: Lawrence Erlbaum.

Selye, H. (1974). *Stress without distress*. Philadelphia: J.B. Lippincott.

Selye, H. (1976). *The stress of life*. New York: McGraw-Hill.

Sewell, James D. (1981). "Police stress." *FBI Law Enforcement Bulletin*, April.

Solomon, R.M. (1988). "Post-shooting trauma." *Police Chief*, October, pp. 40–44.

Spielberger, C.D. et al. (1981). *The police stress survey: sources of stress in law enforcement.* Tampa: University of Southern Florida, College of Social and Behavioral Sciences. (Human Resources Institute Monograph series 3, no. 6).

Stratton, J. (1978). "Police stress: an overview." *Police Chief*, Vol. 45, no. 4 (April), pp. 58–62.

Stratton, J.G., D.A. Parker, and J.R. Snibbe (1984). "Post-traumatic stress: study of police officers involved in shooting." *Psychological Reports*, Vol. 55, pp. 127–131.

Terry, W. Clinton III (1981). "Police stress: the empirical evidence." *Journal of Police Science and Administration*, Vol. 9, pp. 61–74.

Terry, W. Clinton III (1985). "Police stress as a professional self-image." *Journal of Criminal Justice*, Vol. 13, pp. 501–512.

Vila, Bryan (2000). *Tired cops: the importance of managing police fatigue*. Washington, D.C.: Police Executive Research Forum.

Violanti, J.M. (1983). "Stress patterns in police work: a longitudinal study." *Journal of Police Science and Administration*, Vol. 11, pp. 211–216.

Violanti, J.M. (1996). "Violence turned inward: police suicide in the workplace." In VandenBos, G.R. and E.Q. Bulatao (eds.) *Violence on the job: identifying risks and developing solutions*. Washington, D.C.: American Psychological Association.

WEBLINKS

 www.css.to/sleep/index.htm Being well-rested is important for police officers, who must be alert and ready to move at a moment's notice. Visit the Canadian Sleep Society's website to find information on sleeping well, or to have questions about sleep patterns answered.

 www.geocities.com/~halbrown/links.html The Police Stress Links website provides numerous links to sites that focus on the issue of police stress or contain significant information related to this topic. The description of each site will help you to find the sites most relevant to your search.

 www.dstress.com/stress.phys.html Sometimes people can be stressed without even realizing it. To learn about the ways your body responds to stress, visit the Stress Education Center's *Physiology of Stress*.

 www.dstress.com/10-tips.htm Now that you've learned about the symptoms of stress from the *Physiology of Stress*, visit the Stress Education Center's list of 10 tips to prevent and reduce stress.

http://web.ukonline.co.uk/bjlogie Directed towards the law enforcement profession in the UK, the Police Shift Work Guide provides detailed information on the effects of shift work in law enforcement and how to be a healthy shift worker.

 www.ncjrs.org/pdffiles1/jr000242d.pdf Go to page 21 of the National Institute of Justice's Journal to learn how stress affects your American counterparts.

APPENDIX A

IACP Administrative Guidelines for Dealing with Officers Involved in On-Duty Shooting Situations*

Police Psychological Services Section

International Association of Chiefs of Police

In the past, officers involved in on-duty shootings were often subjected to a harsh administrative/investigative/legal aftermath that compounded the stress of using deadly force. A "second injury" can be created by insensitively and impersonally dealing with an officer who has been involved in a critical incident.* Due partly to such treatment, many officers have left law enforcement prematurely, as victims.

To minimize emotional problems, the Police Psychological Services Section of IACP has adopted guidelines for dealing with officers involved in a shooting. The guidelines were first submitted to the section by the author in 1987 at the section meeting at the IACP conference in Toronto. After discussion and the making of some changes, the guidelines were preliminarily adopted. At the 1988 section meeting, they were approved as presented below.

The goals of these guidelines is to provide information on how to constructively support the officer(s) involved in a shooting in order to diminish emotional trauma. Extensive field experience has shown that following these guidelines reduces the probability of long-lasting emotional problems resulting from a shooting. However, these guidelines are not meant to be a rigid protocol. It is important to apply these guidelines in a flexible manner that is appropriate to the situation.

1. At the scene, show concern. Give physical *and* mental first aid.

2. Create a psychological break; get the officer away from the body and some distance from the scene. The officer should remain with a supportive peer or supervisor and return to the scene only if necessary. This break should be of a non-stimulant nature, with discretionary use of drinks with caffeine.

3. Explain to the officer what will happen administratively during the next few hours and why, so he does not take the investigation as a personal attack.

4. If the gun is taken as evidence, replace it immediately or when appropriate (with the officer being told it will be replaced). This guideline can be modified depending on how aggravated the circumstances are and how stressed the officer is, e.g. very depressed, agitated, suicidal, etc.

5. The officer should be advised to consider retaining an attorney to watch out for his personal interests.

6. The officer should have some recovery time before detailed interviewing begins. The officer should be in a secure setting, insulated from the press and curious officers.

7. Totally isolating the officer breeds feelings of resentment and alienation. The officer can be with a supportive friend or a peer who has been through a similar experience. (To avoid legal complications, the situation should not

---

*Roger M. Solomon, "Post-Shooting Trauma," *The Police Chief*, October 1988, pp. 40-44

be discussed prior to the preliminary investigation.) It is important to show concern and support to the officer during this time.

8. If the officer is not injured, either he/she or the department should contact the family with a phone call or personal visit and let them know what happened before rumors from other sources reach them. If the officer is injured, a department member known to the family should pick them up and drive them to the hospital. Call friends, chaplains, etc., to make sure they have support.

9. Personal concern and support for the officer involved in the shooting, communicated face-to-face from a high-ranking administrator, goes a long way toward alleviating future emotional problems. The administrator does not have to comment on the situation or make any premature statements regarding legal or departmental resolution, but can show concern and empathy for the officer during this very stressful experience.

10. The officer should be given some *administrative leave* (not suspended with pay) to deal with the emotional impact. (Three days, more or less as the situation dictates, is usually sufficient.) Some officers, however, prefer light duty to leave. Depending on the situation and the officer's reactions, it may be best to keep him off the street temporarily and avoid the double-bind situation of the officer's going back to work and facing the possibility of another critical incident before the investigation, grand jury hearing, coroner's inquest, and district attorney's statement have been completed.

All personnel at the scene (including dispatchers) should be screened for their reactions and given leave or the rest of the shift off, as necessary.

11. To defuse the stigma of seeking counseling, there should be a *mandatory* confidential debriefing with a licensed mental health professional experienced with the law enforcement culture and trauma, prior to returning to duty. This debriefing should be held as soon after the incident as practical. Return to duty and/or follow-up sessions should be determined by the mental health professional.

Everybody at the scene, including the dispatcher, should have a debriefing with the mental health professional within 72 hours. While this can be a group session, the officer(s) who did the shooting may or may not want to be included in the group debriefing, as actually doing the shooting creates different emotional issues. Follow-up sessions for other personnel involved in the shooting may be appropriate.

12. Opportunities for family counseling (spouse, children, significant others) should be made available.

13. If the officer's phone number is published, it may be advisable to have a friend or telephone answering machine screen phone calls, since there are sometimes threats to the officer and his family.

14. An administrator should tell the rest of the department (or the supervisor, the rest of the team) what happened so the officer does not get bombarded with questions and rumors are held in check. Screen for "vicarious thrill seekers."

15. Expedite the completion of administrative and criminal investigations and advisement of the outcomes to the officer.

16. Consider the officer's interests in preparing the media releases.

17. The option of talking to peers who have had a similar experience can be quite helpful to all personnel at the scene. Peer counselors are an asset in conducting group debriefings, in conjunction with a mental health professional, and in providing follow-up support.

18. Allow a paced return to duty; that is, the officer can ride around with a fellow officer or perhaps work a different beat or shift.

To prevent such incidents in the first place, train all officers in critical incident reactions and what to expect personally, departmentally, and legally.

APPENDIX B

IACP Model Policy, Post-Shooting Incident Procedures

POST-SHOOTING
INCIDENT PROCEDURES

Model Policy

Effective Date May 1, 1950	Number

Subject **Post-Shooting Incident Procedures**	

Reference	Special Instructions

Distribution	Reevaluation Date April 30, 1991	No. Pages 2

I. PURPOSE

The purpose of this policy is to provide guidelines that shall be uniformly applied following any officer-involved shooting incident that has resulted in death or serious bodily injury, in order to minimize the chances that involved personnel will develop or suffer from post-traumatic stress disorder.

II. POLICY

Law enforcement duties can often expose officers and support personnel to mentally painful and highly stressful situations that cannot be resolved through normal stress coping mechanisms. Unless adequately treated, these situations can cause disabling emotional and physical problems. It has been

The development of this model policy was supported under funding by the U.S. Department of Justice's Bureau of Justice Assistance under Grant No. 87-SN-CX-K077. The points of view or opinions stated in this document are the results of work performed by the International Association of Chiefs of Police and do not necessarily reflect the official position or policies of the U.S. Department of Justice.

found that officer-involved shootings resulting in death or serious bodily injury to a citizen or a fellow officer may precipitate such stress disorders. It is the responsibility of this law enforcement agency to provide personnel with information on stress disorders and to guide and assist in their deterrence. Therefore, it should be the policy of this agency to take immediate action after such incidents to safeguard the continued good mental health of all involved personnel.

III. DEFINITIONS
   A. Post-Traumatic Stress Disorder: An anxiety disorder that can result from exposure to short-term severe stress or the long-term buildup of repetitive and prolonged milder stress.
   B. Officer-Involved Shooting Incident: A line-of-duty incident when shooting causes death or serious bodily injury to an officer or other person.

IV. PROCEDURES
   A. Handling of Officers at Scene of Shooting Incident
      1. A supervisor shall be dispatched to the scene of the incident, and shall assume primary responsibility for caring for involved personnel.
      2. The supervisor shall make appropriate arrangements for all necessary medical treatment.
      3. During any period where the involved officer is required to remain on the scene, but has no immediate duties to fulfil, the officer should be taken to a quiet area away from the scene of the incident. A peer counselor or other supportive friend or officer should remain with the officers, but should be advised not to discuss details of the incident.
      4. The supervisor should arrange for the officers directly involved in the incident to leave the scene as soon as possible, and be taken to a quiet, secure setting.
      5. Where possible, the supervisor shall briefly meet with the involved officers.
         a. No caffeine or other stimulants or depressants should be given to the officers unless administered by medical personnel.
         b. Only minimal, preliminary questions should be asked about the incident. The officers should be advised that a more detailed debriefing will be conducted at a later time.
         c. Any standard investigations that will occur concerning the incident should be discussed with the officers.
         d. The officers should be advised that they may seek legal counsel.
         e. The officers should be advised not to discuss the incident with anyone except a personal or agency attorney, union representative, or departmental investigator, until the conclusion of the preliminary investigation.
      6. The supervisor shall determine whether the circumstances of the incident require that the officer's duty weapon be taken for laboratory analysis. Where the duty weapon is taken, the supervisor shall;
         a. Take custody of the officer's weapon in a discrete [sic] manner; and
         b. Replace it with another weapon, or advise the officer that it will be returned or replaced at a later time, as appropriate.
      7. Involved officers should notify their families about the incident as soon as possible. Where an officer is unable to do so, an agency official shall personally notify his family, and arrange for their transportation to the hospital.
      8. At all times, when at the scene of the incident, the supervisor should handle the officer and all involved personnel in a manner that acknowledges the stress caused by the incident.

   B. Post-Incident Procedures
      1. Involved personnel shall be removed from line duties pending evaluation but shall remain available for any necessary administrative investigations.
      2. All officers directly involved in the shooting incident shall be required to

contact an agency designated specialist for counseling and evaluation as soon as practical after the incident. Involved support personnel should also be encouraged to contact such specialists after a shooting incident. After the counseling sessions, the specialist shall advise the agency:

  a. Whether it would be in the officers' best interest to be placed on administrative leave or light duty, and for how long;
  b. Where the officers were relieved of their duty weapons after an incident, at what point they should be returned;
  c. What will be the best continued course of counseling.

3. The agency strongly encourages the families of the involved officers to take advantage of available counseling service.

4. Any agency investigation of the incident shall be conducted as soon and as quickly as practical.

5. The agency should brief other agency members concerning the incident so that rumors are kept to a minimum. Agency members are encouraged to show the involved officers their concern.

6. All personnel involved in a shooting incident should be advised that they are not permitted to speak with the media about the incident. Officers shall refer inquiries from the media to a designated agency spokesperson, unless otherwise authorized to release a statement pertaining to the incident.

7. In order to protect against crank or abusive calls, officers should be advised to have phone calls answered by another person for several days if their names are released to the public.

8. Officers directly involved in the shooting incident shall be required to requalify as soon as practical.

C. Daily Stress Recognition
1. As post-traumatic stress disorders may not arise immediately, or the officers may attempt to hide the problem, each supervisor is responsible for monitoring the behavior of unit members for symptoms of the disorder. A supervisor may order an officer to seek assistance or counseling from a mental health specialist upon a reasonable belief that stress may be disrupting the officer's job performance.

D. Training
1. The agency shall provide employees with training pertaining to post-traumatic stress disorders and the uniform procedures contained in this policy on a regular basis.

2. Supervisors are responsible for making available to their unit members information about the agency's peer counseling group and mental health services.

BY ORDER OF

_____

CHIEF OF POLICE

The IACP Model Policy on Post-Shooting Incident Procedures was developed under the auspices of the advisory board to the IACP/BJA National Law Enforcement Policy Center. It is intended to serve as a guide for the law enforcement executive who is interested in formulating a written procedure to prevent and resolve potential problems that may result from post-shooting incidents. The law enforcement executive is advised to refer to all federal, state and municipal statutes, ordinances, regulations, and judicial and administrative decisions to ensure that the policy he seeks to implement meets the unique needs of the jurisdiction.

INDEX

LITERARY CREDITS

Chapter 1

Page 2: Quotation excerpted from *Policing Ontario: building for the future: June 8th & 9th, 1996.* Toronto: Ministry of the Solicitor General and Correctional Services.

Pages 3, 7: Quotations excerpted from Leclerc, Guy et al. (1996). *Accountability, performance reporting, comprehensive audit: an integrated perspective.* Ottawa: CCAF-FCVI.

Pages 5–7: Table adapted from Leclerc, Guy et al. (1996). *Accountability, performance reporting, comprehensive audit: an integrated perspective.* Ottawa: CCAF-FCVI.

Pages 8, 19: Quotations excerpted from Bayley, D.H. (1983). "Accountability and control of the police: some lessons for Britain." In Bennett, T. (ed.) *The future of policing: papers presented to the 15th Cropwood Round-Table Conference December 1982.* Cambridge: Institute of Criminology, University of Cambridge.

Page 8: List of possible responsibilities of a governing authority excerpted from Hann, Robert G. et al. (1985). "Municipal police governance and accountability in Canada: an empirical study." *Canadian Police College Journal*, vol. 9, no. 1, pp. 1–85.

Pages 10, 11, 12, 14: Quotations excerpted from Stenning, Philip C. (1981). *Police commissions and boards in Canada.* Toronto: Centre of Criminology, University of Toronto.

Page 18: Table adapted from Oliver, Ian (1987). *Police, government and accountability.* London: The Macmillan Press.

Pages 19–20, 21: Quotations excerpted from Martin, Maurice A. (1995). *Urban Policing in Canada: Anatomy of an Aging Craft.* Montreal and Kingston: McGill-Queen's University Press.

Chapter 2

Page 29: Quotation excerpted from *Policing Ontario: building for the future: June 8th & 9th, 1996.* Toronto: Ministry of the Solicitor General and Correctional Services.

Page 30, 42: Quotation and Figure 2.3 excerpted from Adams, G.W. (1998). *Consultation Report of the Honourable George W. Adams, Q.C. to the Attorney General and Solicitor General Concerning Police Cooperation with the Special Investigations Unit.*

Pages 30, 33: Quotations excerpted and figure adapted from McLeod, Roderick M. (1996). *A report and recommendations on amendments to the* Police Services Act *respecting civilian oversight of Police.* Toronto: Miller Thomson.

Pages 37, 43: Figure 2.2, Table 2.1, and Role of the SIU Investigator used by permission of the Special Investigations Unit (Ontario). Corrections to these items provided by the Special Investigations Unit.

Page 44: Quotation excerpted from Philips, Cyril, (1983). "The police complaints system in England and Wales." In Bennett, T. (ed.) *The future of policing: papers presented to the 15th Cropwood Round-Table Conference December 1982.* Cambridge: Institute of Criminology, University of Cambridge.

Page 44: Quotation excerpted from Lewis, Clare E. (1991). "Police complaints in Metropolitan Toronto: perspectives of the public complaints commissioner." In Goldsmith,

Andrew J. (ed.) *Complaints against the police: the trend to external review*. Oxford: Clarendon Press.

Pages 48, 52, 53, 55, 58, 59, 61, 62, 65: Tables 2.2–2.14 adapted from the Office of the Police Complaint Commissioner (2001).

Pages 57–8: Quotation excerpted from Law Enforcement Review Agency (2000). "What do we investigate?" [online.] [Cited November 20, 2001.] <www.gov.mb.ca/justice/lera/process/process.html>.

Chapter 3

Page 72: Quotation excerpted from Lewis, Clare E. (1991). "Police complaints in Metropolitan Toronto: perspectives of the public complaints commissioner." In Goldsmith, Andrew J. (ed.) *Complaints against the police: the trend to external review*. Oxford: Clarendon Press.

Pages 73, 82: Quotations excerpted from Sheehan, Robert and Gary W. Cordner (1995). Police *administration*.3rd. edition. Cincinnati, Ohio: Anderson Publishing Co.

Pages 73, 74, 77–78, 81: Quotations excerpted from Ontario Civilian Commission on Police Services (1992). *Report of an inquiry into administration of internal investigations by the Metropolitan Toronto Police Force.* Toronto: The Commission.

Page 83: Quotations excerpted from Philips, Cyril, (1983). "The police complaints system in England and Wales." In Bennett, T. (ed.) *The future of policing: papers presented to the 15th Cropwood Round-Table Conference December 1982.* Cambridge: Institute of Criminology, University of Cambridge.

Page 84: Quotation excerpted from the RCMP External Review Committee Mandate. © Her Majesty in Right of Canada 2001. Reproduced with permission, courtesy of the RCMP External Review Committee.

Pages 91–92: Quotation excerpted from Kluge, Eike-Henner W. (1999). *Ethics and policing: opinion of Dr. Eike-Henner W. Kluge: OPCC file #0302.* Victoria, British Columbia: Office of the Police Complaint commissioner.

Pages 92, 93, 94, 95: Figures 3.1–3.4 used by permission of the Canadian Association of Chiefs of Police.

Chapter 4

Page 103: Quotation excerpted from Biro, Fred, Peter Campbell, Paul McKenna, and Tonita Murray (2000) *Police executives under pressure: a study and discussion of the issues.* Ottawa: Canadian Association of Chiefs of Police. (Police Futures Group; study series no.3.)

Page 104: Quotations excerpted from Forcese, Dennis (1992). *Policing Canadian society*. Scarboroough, Ontario: Prentice-Hall Canada.

Pages 112-113: Quotation excerpted from CPA Services, Core Values and Strategies. <www.cpa-acp.ca>.

Chapter 5

Pages 123, 124: Table 5.1 and Table 5.2 used by permission of the Minister of Industry, as Minister responsible for Statistics Canada. Information on the availability of the wide range of data from Statistics Canada can be obtained from Statistics Canada Regional Offices, its World Wide Web site at *www.statcan.ca*, and its toll free access number 1-800-263-1136.

Page 126–127: Quotation used by permission of the First Nations Chiefs of Police Association (1992).<www.soonet.ca/fncpa>.

Page 127: Quotation excerpted from Clairmont, D. and C.J. Murphy (2000). *Self-administered First Nations' Policing: an overview of organizational and management issues.* Ottawa: Solicitor General Canada. Reproduced with permission of the Minister of Public works and Government Services Canada, 2001.

Chapter 6

Page 133, 134: Quotation excerpted from Canadian Association of Chiefs of Police. Human Resources Committee (2001). *Canadian Association of Chiefs of Police 2001 Annual Report: CACP presents a national use of force framework.* Ottawa: Canadian Association of Chiefs of Police.

Page 134: Figure 6.1 (National Use of Force Framework) excerpted from CACP Newsletter, vol. 20, no. 1 &2 (Spring/ Summer), p. 12. Used by permission of the Canadian Association of Chiefs of Police.

Page 136: Table 6.1 (Extent of Departmental Attention to Different Types of Use of Force Issues) excerpted from Geller, William A. and Hans Toch (eds.) *And justice for all: understanding and controlling police abuse of force.* © 1995, Police Executive Research Forum, Washington, D.C. Used with Permission.

Page 138: Table 6.2 (Technical Specifications for Handguns) reprinted by permission of Queen's Printer for Ontario, 2002. © Queen's Printer for Ontario, 2002.

Page 140: Figure 6.2 (Use of Force Report) used by permission of the Queen's Printer for Ontario, 2002. © Queen's Printer for Ontario, 2002.

Chapter 7

Page 150: Table 7.1 (Signs and Symptoms of Stress) adapted from Anderson, Wayne, David Swenson, and Daniel Clay (1995). *Stress management for law enforcement officer.* Englewood Cliffs, New Jersey: Prentice Hall.

Page 153: Table 7.2 (Factors that Influence an Officer's Reactions to a Shooting) excerpted from Anderson, Wayne, David Swenson, and Daniel Clay (1995). *Stress management for law enforcement officer.* Englewood Cliffs, New Jersey: Prentice Hall.

Page 154: Table 7.3 (Stress Management Techniques) adapted from Anderson, Wayne, David Swenson, and Daniel Clay (1995). *Stress management for law enforcement officer.* Englewood Cliffs, New Jersey: Prentice Hall.